APPALACHIAN
REVIEW

VOL. 49, NO. 3
SUMMER 2021

TRADITION. DIVERSITY. CHANGE.

ESTABLISHED IN 1973
PUBLISHED QUARTERLY
by Berea College
www.appalachianreview.net

CONTENTS

INTERVIEW

BOOK REVIEWS

CONTRIBUTORS

COVER PHOTOGRAPH

Juniper Haircut Moss by Jeremy Paden

EDITOR'S NOTE

JASON KYLE HOWARD

When this magazine was founded nearly fifty years ago by the poet Albert Stewart, readers would have been hard-pressed to find quality literature about contemporary Appalachia that was both widely available and consistently published. Such writing existed, to be sure, in the work of writers including Lisa Alther,

Harriette Simpson Arnow, Annie Dillard, Wilma Dykeman, Nikki Giovanni, Jim Wayne Miller, Gurney Norman, Lee Smith, James Still, and others. But the gaps of time between releases was lengthy. Black writers, writers of color, indigenous writers, queer writers, and women writers were all woefully underrepresented.

A few weeks ago, as I was thumbing through a list of new releases and upcoming books focused on Appalachia, I had one of those moments. You know the kind I'm talking about—when the past seems both distant and near, when an epiphany arrives with a shiver. As editor of *Appalachian Review*, I am especially conscious of the editors who preceded me. I think of what the job must have been like for the magazine's earliest editors, Al Stewart and Sidney Saylor Farr. Sometimes, it feels like I have invited them into my office. I wonder how they might have approached a particular situation; I muse about the problems and concerns they would have encountered in their respective work days. An abundance of voices would not have been one of them.

Consider: this summer, and in the months ahead, there will be dozens of literary works published from and about Appalachia—a statistic that would surely have made the eyes of both Stewart and Farr widen, perhaps in disbelief, but certainly in delight. On the fiction horizon, recently published or forthcoming novels and story collections include *When the Ghosts Come Home* by Wiley Cash, *Flight Risk* by Joy Castro, *The Blue Line Down* by Maris Lawyer, *Perpetual West* by Mesha Maren, *Allegiance* by Gurney Norman, *In the Valley* by Ron Rash, *Mother Country* by Jacinda Townsend, and *Drowned Town* by Jayne Moore Waldrop. In creative nonfiction, there is *Southbound* by Anjali Enjeti, *Perfect Dirt* by Keegan Lester, *Voice Lessons* by Karen Salyer McElmurray,

Fierce and Delicate: Essays on Dance and Illness by Renée K. Nicholson, *Kin* by Shawna Kay Rodenberg, and *Paper Concert: A Conversation in the Round* by Amy Wright. Poetry titles include *English Lit* by Bernard Clay, *World as Sacred Burning Heart* by Jeremy Paden, *Perfect Black* by Crystal Wilkinson, *What We Take With Us* by Sylvia Woods, and *The Girl Singer* by Marianne Worthington.

This is an impressive (albeit non-exhaustive) list, and I'm especially proud to have published the work of many of these authors. But more than that, my heart swells to know that the region's literature is in such good hands. That these writers are introducing and reminding readers about all the identities and languages and dialects and ways of being that exist in this complicated, frustrating, beautiful place. We have more, necessary work to do in terms of representation and diversity. But instead of scarcity, there is starting to be bounty.

(On a related note: if you or someone you know is interested in being a book reviewer, please do not hesitate to reach out. Our book reviews editor, Emily Masters, welcomes queries, and we are eager to continue beefing up this section of the magazine.)

In the meantime, may you enjoy the abundance of Appalachian literature accessible in your local bookshop, as well as the harvest that awaits you in these pages. ■

ULTRAVIOLET

RESHMI HEBBAR

If Jaya had been paying closer attention, the tea wouldn't have been necessary. It had seemed like an extreme measure to take, relevant only to those with severe anxiety instead of distracted suburban women like herself. Yet how mild were its effects now, just the amplification of these animal sounds through the windows Nilesh insisted on leaving open since the shutdowns, the chirrups strangely in sync with the forgotten CD playing on her computer, as if the squirrel flicking its tail on the grass was keeping time with Adam Clayton's bass.

"Did you try Jeff's stuff yet?" asked Melanie, Jaya's former supervisor, when she had popped by before the last in-person staff meeting held by their counseling practice that year.

"He gave you some, too? Psilocybin?" Jaya clarified. Her colleague Jeff had wrapped it like a tiny Christmas present, which sat hidden in her top dresser drawer amidst old makeup and birthday cards. Jaya hadn't wanted to admit then that even as a relatively hip woman in her forties who'd never voted Republican, she hadn't planned on sampling it.

Melanie had been studying the latest family photo Jaya had placed against her hutch—one of herself, Nilesh, Kareena, and Raj dressed up for Diwali and squinting in their front yard. "He claims it's for research purposes," Melanie finally said, lifting her eyebrows. "I'll send everyone some articles about its success in treating PTSD. It's making waves."

As a deeper awareness of the sound layers from the CD began infusing Jaya's mind, what she held onto from that moment in February was how envious of Melanie she had been. Melanie, so poised in her worsted wool skirts, her full blonde hair with gray only visible in it from less than five feet away. Her toneless neutrality. Is that what had made Jaya finally take it—wanting to appear cooler? Was she no better than a peer-pressured teen?

Jaya sat now on the bed in her guest room with the artifacts from the attic spread all around, the grind of a lawn mower and the calls of industrious birds outside forming a strange synesthetic web in which she was suspended and waiting for something more to happen. *God, listen to that!* she told herself. This song was so good. How could she have packed U2 up in the attic? What were those rising notes The

Edge was playing? She had no idea. She hadn't touched a violin since entering high school, which had saddened her mother just like her own teenaged children were doing today to Jaya. What was happening here? Wait.

She felt like dancing. Not the kind of dancing Kareena knew about, or the viral trends Raj performed in the kitchen, his right elbow flapping as he chanted, "I got a new Glock and do a dance with it." At which point Jaya would interject.

"Raj, what are you saying? A Glock!"

"Mother, chill."

Jaya was trying to be lucid now, trying to follow her memories back even as the mushroom should have been kicking in. As if her real reason for indulging in this illicit experience wasn't the very thing she needed to take a break from, her problem with Kareena, which was pinned to her mind like a hair accessory Jaya had been forced to wear against her will, as if she and not Kareena were the child. Kareena and her enormous wall of photos of herself standing in a line of blonde and dirty blonde girls making duck lips. Kareena and her requests to go early to and stay late at these blonde friends' houses before and after football and basketball games. Kareena and her pouting responses whenever Jaya hollered up the stairs for her to wake up so she wouldn't miss dance practice on the mornings after those late night gatherings at her friends' houses. Kareena shirking the same extra bharatanatyam classes she'd begged for a year before, after talking her parents out of their reservations about the expense of an arangetram, a formal recital demonstrating mastery in Indian classical dance. Which was the last thing Kareena appeared to care about anymore.

So that's it? That's the reason you took drugs? Nilesh's voice accosted Jaya in her head now. He was Indian but born and raised in the States like Jaya, though his parents weren't from the part of the motherland that thought classical dance was important. But her husband and the kids were out for the day, so she shouldn't have been hearing any voices. He'd urged them to accompany him on a two-hour journey across the state line to pick up a gently used Peloton bike in Birmingham.

"Why can't Mom go with you?" Raj had asked.

"Because she's going to clean out the attic," Nilesh had answered, "and because I'd like some personal time with the two of you."

"God!" Kareena had exclaimed.

Nilesh was too well-adjusted a person to understand how a fifteen-year-old girl's behavior could trigger her mother's experiment with hallucinogens. He still thought psychology and therapy were for people who took remedial math instead of advanced calculus. But he was also the type of husband who

Jaya had hoped when her children grew up they would find someone like him to be with, someone who recognized them, even if that person wasn't able to get them all of the time.

said, "Don't worry if you don't get much of the attic done. It's fine if we come back and find you crashed in front of a Reese Witherspoon movie." Jaya had hoped when her children grew up they would find someone like him to be with, someone who recognized them, even if that person wasn't able to get them all of the time. Even if Kareena couldn't yet see how important shared cultural backgrounds were.

Jaya needed to go downstairs while she was still herself and retrieve the teacup before she forgot about it and it was discovered there on the counter. "Make a tea with it," Jeff had suggested when he'd slipped the tiny box into her hand during their office holiday party. "High tea," she had joked and immediately felt like a poseur when Jeff had roared.

How bright it was downstairs, and how lovely was their home! They'd been shut up for so long that she'd not had a chance to appreciate its warmth, the windows in the front and back framing the maturing shrubs and trees. Without the soundtrack of pop music, the outdoor activity was somehow sharper. Footsteps near the house seemed to crash nearby, and yet upon examination, it was only a pack of blue jays scavenging in the backyard. Jaya found the vanilla-colored cup and held it carefully in her hand. Nothing had really happened yet; but all the literature Melanie had shared with the practice on the debate about using psilocybin in psycho-therapy had emphasized its mind-altering abilities. Jaya took an extra gulp and went and sat at the island, where in March, a week before everyone had been sent home, Kareena had asked her parents if she could dye six inches of her hair purple.

"It seems reasonable, right?" Nilesh had said in their bedroom. "Maybe we can incentivize her somehow. If she does *blank* then she'll get purple hair."

"You don't think it's a little too..." Jaya couldn't finish.

"Too what?"

But Jaya couldn't say it.

"Hey, Barney!" Raj sang out whenever he saw his older sister, alluding to the simple-minded friendly dinosaur of a simpler time.

So Jaya had stalled until Kareena came and found her one morning perched on the front step watching the residents of their subdivision walk by in the cavalcades that had begun after the gyms had closed down.

"Don't you have work?" Kareena had asked, sitting next to her with a bowl of cereal in her hands.

"I'm doing a video session upstairs in an hour."

"Don't people feel weird about that?"

Jaya had looked at her daughter. Sometimes Kareena's questions were surprisingly canny.

"Yes," Jaya admitted. "But we all have to make do, right?"

What was it about being a parent that made it so difficult to have a conversation without a moral attached?

Then Kareena had dropped the pretense of casualness and followed-up about wanting permission to dye her hair. And Jaya had cowardly asked her daughter what it would look like to have a girl with purple hair performing an arangetram. Kareena had stood up with her bowl and retreated through the front door, which had a way of slamming whether or not the person intended it. Jaya remembered this now in her kitchen and wondered if she went and sat on her front step whether her neighbors would be able to tell that she had consumed a magic mushroom. Something wailed distantly outside, and when Jaya scrambled for the doorknob to the back deck so she could take a look, she saw what appeared to be a mustache confidently circling the blue sky. What did the mustache remind her of? How could a mustache be in the sky?

Uh-oh.

The sunlight appeared to be following her, breaking and entering through the transom at the front door, creating an effect that looked a bit too much like Superman's birthplace. *I was just on these stairs,* Jaya thought, *climbing and climbing.* That was just now. Was this really happening? Or was she reading about it? And, oh, the soft gray of the hallway upstairs and the music again, still going, nearing the end of the album, Jaya could tell, because some things you never forgot, even after three decades, like how Bono smoldered in the "With or Without You" video, which was released years before this disc playing now, and from *The Joshua Tree*, but still. Connections. Because Jaya, in a rare show of sharing with her mother, had once told her, "I want to marry someone like that someday," meaning Bono, and her mother had responded so sincerely that it had stuck with Jaya: "I don't know where I'm going to find you an Indian boy like that."

Had Jaya been serious back then? Probably not. Nilesh couldn't sing. And he looked down on men with ponytails.

Did that mean that Kareena hadn't been serious when she'd said what she'd said?

How nice it was that Kareena left her bedroom door open before departing with her father, as if inviting her mother to come in and lie down on the floor. "Baby, baby, baby," crooned Bono from the next room, and Jaya thought, yes, that's who Kareena still was, even though most of the time her door remained closed, which felt like a slap in Jaya's face. How many months now had it been since her daughter started behaving as if everyone was against her, that Jaya had been trying to control her, and the pandemic had been specifically generated to squash her attempts to see her friends?

"Can I ask," Jaya had finally felt brave enough to try one day months ago, "what's the significance of all these photos on the wall?"

Kareena's nostrils had widened. "What do you mean? God!"

"Calm down, sweetheart. I just want to know what you're trying to say."

"I'm not trying to say anything! These are my friends. They make me happy."

And Jaya had wanted to ask, *are you sure about that?* She wanted to tell Kareena that for the best times of her own life, moments that had taught her who she was and who she wanted to be, she had no photos, just fragments of things stuffed in boxes that eventually got put in the attic. But like the therapist she was, Jaya said nothing and waited. Then she told

Kareena that putting tape all over the walls risked pulling off the paint.

Now here were those walls, still perfectly mauve, the color of fashionable eyeshadow. They formed a soothing counterpoint to the neon flashing from Kareena's laptop screensaver, the ribbons of yellow, green, blue, and pink zipping through the air like invisible gymnasts were practicing floor exercises across her desk. Point. Counterpoint. Mustache to acrobatic ribbons. The CD was starting over again on Jaya's computer in the guest room because she had been clearheaded enough then to set it to repeat. Probably because it was the only CD she still owned. Her phone was better downstairs, where people couldn't get to her. And who wanted YouTube ads to ruin this psychic experience? If it really turned out to be something.

Jeff had texted Jaya back with tips that morning when she'd texted that she was ready to have some tea: "Listen to some music! Look at a painting!" And she'd wanted to respond back, *What do you think this is? Just getting my family out of the house is an adventure.* The only "painting" she'd had a chance to look at was the old print of Lord Krishna and his admirers, the Gopis, which Jaya's parents had foisted on her when they'd downsized. It was still sitting up there in the attic, next to where her old shoeboxes full of notebooks and one CD had been. Honestly, that's what these screensaver colors looked like as she lay on her back on Kareena's carpet. Forget acrobats. They were silk and chiffon dupattas trailing from the necks of all the women who danced and chased Lord Krishna around a field in that old print.

Oh, the greenness of that field, the same color of the leaves stirring outside Kareena's open window. Bless Nilesh for doing this every morning, forcing his children to look outside, to notice the surprising tranquility there despite evidence to the contrary in the news, the red crowned microbes that were turning everything upside down, even without the aid of mushrooms. And, yes, there are a few yellow leaves already—it was August—and, no, there wouldn't be a festival season this year, no dancing like the Gopis at Navratri in some indoor hall, thousands of Indian people together to remind Kareena and Raj of who they were. Which was one more thing gone this year besides what Nilesh had mentioned in July, when he asked Jaya if she had reached out to the proprietors of the hall where Kareena was slated to perform her arangetram in a few months, going as she still was to most weekend practices, standing masked at the far end of the studio away from her guru.

"If things keep up like this, I don't see anyone wanting to come to an indoor dance recital in October," Nilesh had said before Jaya had broken down.

But why did she need to go to that moment when she could release herself to this green field, the sunlight pulling itself up over the roof and punching its way through the open

But why did she need to go to that moment when she could release herself to this green field, the sunlight pulling itself up over the roof and punching its way through the open windows...

windows like a superhero, illuminating the strange mixing of birds, cardinals with robins with sparrows gathering in the dogwood trees to the right of Kareena's other window, like they were all at a rest stop on the way to somewhere else, and it didn't matter anymore which family they belonged to, which group? All they wanted was a necessary break from flight.

Jaya closed her eyes, stretched out her arms, and fell through the web of music, light, and memory. Without landing exactly, she saw the field of Gopis transformed to so many people, her parents, her children, Kareena in the expensive green performance outfit they'd ordered for her from Bombay, her eyes wide and head cocked to one side as if beginning a bharatanatyam dance, Raj next to her in a rap stance, the gelled peaks of his hair moving in time to the music guiding the circle, the Indian friends who usually attended the fall festivals with their family. There they all were, Nilesh in a gorgeous blue sherwani, and so many others from her life, her brother and his latest white girlfriend, and even her old Hindu temple camp friends, but it was like a dream, so she couldn't be sure if she was seeing the teens they had all been, or the adults she might have known now if she had stayed in touch with them. And she could not believe how powerful the light was, and she could not be sure whether it was really filtering from the maples and dogwoods outside, or was something created in her mind, as the field transformed from day to night, turning to a bonfire—was this a reference to the spring festival of Hoi? Was Jaya really there? Then the bonfire seemed to fall to ash and back into a field, a different one this time, spread over with flowers that were impossibly varied, light purples and oranges, the petals and stems as defined as the fingers of dancers in motion. Jaya realized they were the wildflowers of fields in Pennsylvania, which she'd marveled at when she'd been there for that brief time at temple camp, pointing them out to the other girls, who'd thought she'd been making a big deal about nothing.

"Why do you care about wildflowers when you live right next to a beach?" Jaya remembered her sophisticated roommate at camp, Anita, asking her.

Because you guys don't have to live down there with people who don't know what a temple is,

Jaya should have said. Screw the beach. I belong here with you. With these flowers in this field.

But now something else was happening to the vision, and Jaya could tell it was happening, as if she were turning a page in a book, which meant that the tea couldn't have been that strong, and yet she couldn't stop herself from turning it. Heavy. She felt a heavy, dreamy languor come over her there in the patch of sunlit carpet, underneath the photo wall of blond and dirty blonde teenagers she was still too chicken to talk honestly about with her daughter. To tell her, *sweetheart, you'll never be one of them. You need to be with your own people.*

Yet Kareena had guessed anyway. During that painful conversation about the photos, she had snarled at Jaya: "I hope you don't expect me to marry someone Indian!" How had her daughter got that from Jaya's innocent question about whether Kareena had any Indian friends? But it was true. It was true. Had Jaya's own mother ever felt this? Well, it was a moot point because Jaya had ultimately done everything right for herself. There were no regrets. No holes to fill.

She was for some reason now away from the field and in a classroom. Strange. Was this supposed to be Kareena's vision? Had the psilocybin initiated one of those *Freaky Friday* moments so that Jaya could go back and see what it was like to be fifteen?

But this wasn't a school. The light was falling on smooth conference tables spread in a "U" shape, at the head of which an Indian man in a mustache—mustache!—was glowering at them. Oh, she was back here. Back at temple camp, inside the lecture room, sitting next to her old Indian friends and across from Arjun, all of whom she had no photos of. She'd fallen in love with them all, not just Arjun, Pallavi's cute and crazy twin brother. All of them, the sense they had made together that first time in Jaya's life when she had felt she belonged somewhere. Yes, they were all there, only their faces were the incongruous ones of dreams, as if the vision was telling Jaya more about her memory than about reality. Arjun was raising his hand so that the man with the mustache, a teacher or spiritual leader whose name Jaya couldn't remember, would call on him. Which he did.

"Sometimes when I look at the trees… " Arjun began.

"Yes?" The man with the mustache seemed impatient.

"It's like there's a white light coming off of them. Like I can see the white part of the light reflecting off the green leaves."

"Ah," the teacher said after a moment.

"What are you on, Arjun?" one of the other boys around him teased, and then there was so much laughter, and Jaya was pretty sure this had actually happened, that she had laughed too, but inside she had been thinking, *I get it! I know what you mean.*

Had she finally opened her eyes now? Were the maples and dogwoods through the window really bobbing in time to "Ultraviolet (Light My Way)"? How could that song be playing again? How much time had passed? Oh, the sweet release of ambiguity. How wonderful it was to lie here and be taken to wherever her unconscious wanted to go. Why did she have to be swept away now, like she had turned *into* one of the scarves in the hands of the dancers around Krishna in the old print, back on the field but somehow rising above it, into the clouds, so that each gaseous molecule was visible? So that each particle of white pulled apart from the whole, destroying the sense that they were full clouds. She was up here with the birds looking down on the dancers. Only the birds were singing in English along with Bono, and from this height, Jaya saw how much blank space there was in between the field and the dancers, blank space between their faces and their limbs, as if in the patterns created by light passing overhead, she was suddenly compelled to focus on where it did not fall.

More people were there on the field, too. People Jaya had gone to school with and forgotten about, people she saw at work, like Jeff and Melanie, people who lived on their street, so that she could no longer locate where her little foursome was, the one she had created with Nilesh, whose integrity she had hoped would stand the test of generations to come, after her children married Indian people like she and he had done, so that they would always have security, which was protection against the hollowness people like Jaya sometimes felt in their adult lives. *Why should that be?* a bird with a mustache seemed to be asking her. *How can you be hollow if you've done everything to keep yourself whole?*

Now she floated downwards. She was in the dancers' circle with them, everyone irradiating so that the hair and skin color of people like Jaya's childhood friends, and the hair and skin color of Jaya's extended family members was leached away into the dark amber color of evening on the field, until all the people it seemed who had ever been in her life took on a glow

Now she floated downwards. She was in the dancers' circle with them, everyone irradiating...

of the ages. Maybe it was that Jaya had missed dancing like this. Or maybe it was that she missed people. Either way, she found that it no longer mattered to her that she couldn't figure out who she was or where she was in the circle. She didn't know if she was the person she had once been, or the person she had wanted to be, or the person she actually was. She only knew that she was somewhere in between, whether reflected, or wholly seen, or imagined.

"Maya is illusion," the teacher man from temple camp boomed in her head now. Jaya's eyes were closed, only blankness there. She could see nothing, which was a gift. "And everything is maya."

Jaya felt someone who might be her smile now. Maybe it was her getting up, or maybe it was someone in a dream, but it definitely wasn't the person who had sobbed in bed with Nilesh weeks before, after he'd hinted that there could be no arangetram in this time of social distancing, that they needed to get their check back for the deposit on the hall. Testing the limits of his emotional intelligence, she'd stammered at him.

"What's going to happen to everything?"

"Jaya, they're going to find a vaccine. We're being as safe as we can," he had reasoned.

"No. This! All of this!" She'd waved her hands around, wanting to indicate the photos on her dresser of herself and Nilesh at their wedding, wishing to include the traditional outfits embroidered in gold thread hanging at the back of her closet in dry-cleaning bags, all the brightly hued dupattas, circling her hand back between herself and him, until she had to admit that her gestures weren't making sense. "What's going to happen to everything we've known and taught them when they grow up and end up with white people?"

"Come on, Jaya," Nilesh had finally answered. "It's not that simple." Then, because there were no other conclusions to be found, they'd held each other in the light of the nightstand lamps.

Whoever it was now speaking in her head was telling her to get back to the guest room, to get out of here before her daughter found her in an altered state of mind on her floor. Jaya found herself in the guest room reexamining those things from the past that had been spread out on the bed: an old autograph book, report cards, and the small legal pad of lecture notes on Hindu philosophy taken at temple camp. Hours ago, after she'd reasoned that if she pulled a few boxes from the attic she could take Nilesh up on his offer to let her just relax for the whole day, she'd found it in a shoebox. On the notepad's first page were phrases scrawled in the script of teenage experimentation: "Happiness, Awareness, Love, Relax." She'd found another sheet with faint addresses written across it, the names and towns for Anita and the others, girls whose parents had all held the same expectations, girls whose regular social worlds had been similarly dominated by blonde kids, girls whose identities had been decoupaged with American longings and imperfect engagements with whatever it meant to be Indian.

None of them had ever attempted to contact Jaya after that first year of writing letters. No social media pokes or catch-up emails. It had made things worse, deep down, that she knew this even while she had been hoping her daughter would have a similar experience to make her fall in love with her own people.

The legal pad held half sensible ideas written by a person whom Jaya did not exactly remember being. Like this nugget on the last page, which might have been the real reason she finally decided to open Jeff's gift and make the tea: "Ego is the illusion of a separate self." Under this, like a line of poetry had been annotated, was something else: "A can see the white light of trees."

That palimpsest of discussions about the ego, written thirty years ago but oddly so connected to Jaya's work now, and the mystery of what on earth "A" was. And, oh, the excitement that sparked from her phone when she'd texted Jeff that she was going to try it, so rare a thrill it was now to experience people in her life celebrating her potential, like the feeling she'd gotten when she'd emailed her college friends the weekend after she had first met Nilesh at that mixer, when she had written to them that she was going to call him like he'd asked her to. *Do it,* they'd written. *Do it,* Jeff had texted.

It was a feeling greater and more powerful than the disappointments that life threw at a person, the chief of those being that the moments one held as precious couldn't be seen that way to everybody. How a week that meant so much to her, starved of her own heritage as she had been as a Southern girl, might be nothing special for others who grew up near temples instead of beaches. How the attractions of traditional dance experienced by a young child might simply become boring to that same person as she grows and makes new friends. All of these insights seemed now like things a licensed practitioner should have been able to realize much earlier.

Jaya hit pause on the CD playing on the computer so that her mind could retain some clarity. Then she ejected it and placed it in its case back into the tattered box in which it had been stored. She then walked to the master bedroom where the photo of the four of them in Diwali clothes, which she'd retrieved from her office when it shut down, had been set on her dresser. Working slowly, as if each step was miraculous, she took the photo and went back to grab the small notepad she had discovered. These she held and entered Kareena's room again, the weight of the light still with and on her, the sensation of being moved by a force beyond her seeming like freedom. She placed the photo on Kareena's still humming laptop. Then, she tore out a blank page in the old notepad and wrote with a pen from the desk, "For your photo wall, if you want it. You look beautiful in all the shots."

Jaya resolved to go downstairs now and find a romantic comedy to put on in the background, while the effects of whatever this was slowly left her system. As she turned to go, her attention was caught by a hawk swooping over the trees in her neighbor's backyard, angling and coasting, it seemed to her, like a conductor's baton, causing notes from The Edge's guitar to swell up in a disconcerting way. But the music had been turned off, which meant it must have just been a trick of the mind. ■

FEASTING

Bryce Canyon, August 2019

Stars have a habit of pushing things / away I read
in an article that the Milky Way is a thief taking one breath
and then another keeping / it all I think she likes this
version of herself / stretched wide over this canyon
where I stand at the bottom staring into her / I have never seen
her / like this before / honeycombed in limestone / siltstone
dolomite if I could tear them down / to make the sky
bigger/ give her more / room to fill / would it end
her expanding / the exhaling pitch / the dark with
always more to swallow when I need / a reason to be hungrier

KATELYN JOY WILKINSON

STRIKING DISTANCE

I have it in me so much nearer home
To scare myself with my own desert places.
                          —Robert Frost

At least you pulled me back this time
                you laugh once   I let go of your arm
                          You're getting better
We watch the rattler   taut across the sand
                pull its dinner face-first into the creosote
        You say *ground squirrel* but all I see
                are the red-brown chipmunks burrowed
                        under my parents' porch   fed
                            fat and happy with birdseed
                                through Midwest winters
                        Supposedly
                            the difference is in the stripes
                        Really
                        I don't care what's being eaten
I just want the warning
            the one
                that Mojave green
        didn't give
when it rose up quiet next to my boot
            sideling
                into our path like a guide
Lucky it was still early
        he hadn't warmed up for the day
                            and I had to believe you
                                were right   you
                        know heat
when pressed against your back

          how   quick
       the desert changes
even as we stare into it
               how   still
it gives us spaces to cling
      crooks in canyon walls to rest and watch
               you move above me
                 climbing waterfall stone
         slick even off-season

each handhold a *yes*   until it isn't

KATELYN JOY WILKINSON

AUBADE AT LATE NIGHT TRAILHEAD WITH TARANTULAS

and my body bouncing in the cab of your truck

      as we fumble unpaved down the loose white rock

the weather *bright* and *sunny* the view *amazing always*

      pulling us out to admire all the adjectives

and the way they whip into dust devils around us

      rustling mesquite honey in its begging for hands

how often you look me in the eyes while we talk

      the trail, not content to slip words sideways

into the sand and hope they breadcrumb Blue Diamond

      for miles and miles—*you could walk all day*

turn around and still see the smoke from last night's fire

      you say—your truck now a spot of gypsum

paused somewhere below us but here

      I can warm all day the softness you want

from my body—the path I will leave

when I am ready to find the way home

KATELYN JOY WILKINSON

TREEBEARD

It now appears that certain trees lower and raise their branches, not only at nightfall or sunrise, but also with shorter periods, such as two hours. It's as if they have an internal heartbeat.

—The Scientific and Medical Network Journal, 2018.

busy as we are
we feel your longing
when you walk by
hands held out
fingering
our
bark

busy as we are
feeding fallen sisters and
brothers lying at our feet
feeding beneath the earth
raising branches skyward
lowering again to
earth each night

busy as we are
you swore we moved
& so we did
in the dark
living moving singing things
Fangorn in Sindarin
baritone tree hearts

thrumming along the trail
wrap your arms around
vibrations that feed
your own heart
put your head
against the bast
as if against

some great beast
whose heat rises
from the loam.

ANDREW K. CLARK

THE SEARCH FOR A DIFFERENT MARVIN GARDENS

ALISON CONDIE JAENICKE

for Osaze O. Osagie,
August 2, 1989 – March 20, 2019

I. Osage

His name suggests to me *Osage orange*, the strange green fruit I collected along the paths of Tudek Park to arrange in clear bowls for the State High girls' tennis banquet. The same high school Osaze graduated from a decade before my daughter, the same Tudek Park where the previous December a college student held a gun to his head and police came with mental health professionals to talk him back. He shot himself anyway, but not to death (eye damage but no brain injuries), and a helicopter flew him to a hospital.

Where he recovered. The university sent alerts in the early morning darkness, warning us all to avoid the park. Where were the warnings this time, in the case of Osaze, when he brandished a knife in his Marvin Gardens apartment and threatened to harm himself and others, when the nearby elementary school got information quickly enough to go on lockdown?

Another name for the *Osage orange* is mock orange. Note that the tree—named by the French after the Osage Indians, who call themselves Wahzhaze—does not bear orange fruit. *Osage orange* fruits have skins the bright green of tennis balls, curved and crenellated with tight, winding ridges like brains. Note that the color of all our brains is the same. Even though my skin is a freckled and tanned color called "white," my brain is the same color Ozaze's was. Gray matter alive appears a flushed delicate pink, a mottled mix of white, black, and red.

II. "Less Than a Handful": Community Action for Osaze Osagie, March 27, 2019

A week after Osaze is shot and killed by a police officer called by the young man's father to serve a mental health warrant, we gather to grieve in a used bookstore's back room, our voices competing with live salsa music out front.

The police say Osaze was struck with "less than a handful" of bullets; we are more than a handful. Most here did not know Osaze, although some, like me, know his mother, or father, but we all know we cannot sit still. His middle school Spanish teacher is here to say he was a pleasant, gentle young man. Mental health professionals, a reporter who was called to the scene, members of the county's Democratic Socialist group, friends of the family, a high school student. Mostly white, some Black. A tall white singer, locally famous as "Miss Melanie," raises her voice to say she is raising two kids of color in nearby Penn's Valley. Her short hair is dyed lavender tonight but has been many colors throughout the years. Another woman seated near her sports purple hair pulled into a loose ponytail, and I think of Prince, who sang of purple rain, who explained the song this way: "When there's blood in the sky, red and blue = purple."

At least two other gatherings have sprouted in the past week, one a vigil at the college gates in a cold rain two days after Osaze died, where people under umbrellas shouted outrage, led calls and responses, gripped candles with flames passed tip to tip to allow everyone to meet somebody new. Another gathering was held by CCU: Community and Campus in Unity.

In the bookstore, we talk of Sergeant Slayton, brought in from the two-hour distant state capital, Harrisburg. His job: to reduce tension, manage the situation. Sergeant Slayton says, Be patient, trust the process, we'll tell it like it is.

Someone chimes in: His role is to set the narrative, determine whether violence is justifiable. His role is to pacify and defend. He insults when he says the trend in our country of police shooting young black men doesn't connect with this.

Someone else says: As a seamstress, you cut a pattern, you know how it's going to turn out. Slayton controls the narrative with a pattern of civility. You know what happens with a pattern. What can we do differently to change the pattern?

Then voices spill over each other to be heard:

In this community we call it a "warrant" and other places a "wellness check."

In Phoenix, the mental health squad dresses in casual clothing.

In Eugene, Oregon, they don't send police for a mental health call—they send mental health professionals instead.

Is it true the father called the day before? someone asks.

Yes, it's in the police report, the reporter confirms. They had an entire day to prepare.

It's embarrassing not to have a person of color in the ranks of the borough police force. We need to recruit a person of color to the police force.

And then a tall Black man with dreadlocks speaks from the back: Can we ask Freddie Gray whether it felt better to have his spine snapped by a Black police officer than a white police officer? No, we can't. Because he's dead.

When asked his name, he says, just call me Ray.

Ray tells us what bothers him most is protocol. He speaks as if facing the officers: On your drive there, how the hell did you not go in expecting the worst—a knife, a gun, a conflict? Too many things you could have meditated on, too many ways to go in and help a person.

The taser, what about the taser? someone else asks.

I think they had one, another says.

Sometimes you can "taze" somebody and it doesn't catch.

Ray again: I done seen alligators arrested unharmed. I done seen white people arrested unharmed. I'm kinda tired of making room for the officer to wiggle out. Why no response from the university? Why no Right to Know email or text? If we "All In," we "all in."

Ray wants a spotlight. But he also knows: All this gonna invite more problems for me. I'm about to stay in my apartment now. More visibility doesn't mean we're safer.

The lavender-haired singer tells of a recent time in Penns Valley when someone went and asked those flying

Confederate flags to take them down. What that led to was more red flags flying. My children can't cover their Blackness, she says.

I don't want us to get ahead of the family.
When the spotlight comes they need to be ready.
The family wants to bury him first.
This is their story.
It's our story, too.
There's no blueprint for this, someone says.
Ray replies: Oh, there's a blueprint.

III. To-Do List

- Do not reinvent the wheel.
- Pick up the baton of the task force and move it farther along.
- Contact journalists. Contact the DA. Contact the university president.
- Push for body cams, not just dash cams.
- Read the book *To Protect and Serve*.
- Question. Grieve. Heal. Connect. Pray.
- Amplify the case.
- Prepare for potential backlash.
- Say his name: Osaze.

In Egyptian, the meaning of Osaze is "loved by God."
In Nigerian, Osaze means "the one God chooses."
We say *Osaze*, but never enough.
We say:

> *Osaze.*
> *Dear one.*
> *One of us.*
> *One of our own.*

IV. Epilogue: What's Past is Prologue

Until a few years ago, Osaze's mother was a professor in the English Department; her office was across the hall from mine. In late March 2019, the department sends out details of the family's celebration of life, burial, and repast. I do not go.

In April, I receive a receipt for my donation to the university's Osaze Osagie Memorial Scholarship fund.

In August, the local paper reports: "On the eve of the five-month anniversary of Osaze Osagie's death by State College police shooting, the department released its internal review of the incident and cleared the involved officers of any wrongdoing."

Protests ensue. The family plans to sue.

In November, organizers pull together a three-day art exhibit in a student center art gallery titled "Osaze Was a Freedom Fighter." The closing ceremony will feature singers, poets, and an art curator, with an open discussion afterward.

In May 2020, when George Floyd dies under the knee of police officer Derek Chauvin on a Minneapolis street and the world's cities erupt in shouts and shattered glass and flames, Osaze's name is still on yard signs in our neighborhood. *Remember him*, they say.

On the last day of May, Pentecost Sunday, a peaceful protest on the streets of downtown State College draws a crowd of over 1,000 people. Our university president has issued a statement condemning Floyd's death and supporting the protest. On this day, after more than two months of quarantining with us in the safety of our home, our twenty-one-year-old daughter is driving from State College toward Saint Paul, Minnesota, to move into a house where she will live during her senior year of college.

I do not go to our Pentecost church service, held downtown in our empty church, delivered virtually due to the pandemic, and I do not go to the protest, which brings people together live downtown, masked but in close proximity. I do not see people lying down on the streets; I do not see that "some signs carried the name of Osaze Osagie, the twenty-nine-year-old who was fatally shot by a State College police officer in March 2019."

Instead, I watch and read about both the protest and church service the next day. Instead, I stay home and in touch with our daughter by phone. I fret as she and her housemates decide to delay their arrival into the Twin Cities by a day after hearing reports that white supremacists have been driving around her neighborhood shooting into student houses with Black Lives Matter signs in their windows.

How long will we have to hold up signs, hold out hope, hold such a long string of names in our mouths until none of us can breathe?

The next Sunday, I make a sign from cardboard. I paint it white and write on it with black marker. *Say their names*, it reads. *Osaze, Breonna, George.* "Less Than a Handful" has

How long will we have to hold up signs, hold out hope, hold such a long string of names in our mouths until none of us can breathe?

become "The 3/20 Coalition," named for the date Osaze died in 2019, and they are bringing protestors together in our college town most every week. I drive downtown and join them on the first Sunday after Pentecost.

In Minnesota, our daughter collects money to make supply runs to burned-out neighborhoods in Minneapolis in need of basics: diapers, formula, cleaning supplies, snacks, water. Later in the summer, she dyes her hair purple. She makes paintings of wolves and sell copies through the Twin Cities Makers Collective to raise money for "radical, community-based change."

The 3/20 Coalition presses on through the summer, through Black August and into September. They ask people to send birthday cards to the county DA's office on what would have been Osaze's thirty-first birthday, August 2nd. A birthday Osaze shared with James Baldwin, who wrote: "Not everything that is faced can be changed, but nothing can be changed until it is faced."

September's early days deliver us another name to say— Daniel T. Prude—who like Osaze was Black and mentally unstable, and who, like Osaze, died after family members called for help from police. In March 2020—two months before George Floyd died in the custody of Minneapolis police, one year after Osaze was shot by State College police— in Rochester, New York, police restrained Daniel and placed a spit hood over his head. Lying on the street, naked and handcuffed, the forty-one-year-old man cried, "You're trying to kill me!"

When video showing the encounter is released in September, when the medical report declares his death a homicide due to "complications of asphyxia in the setting of physical restraint," protestors spill into the streets of Rochester and are met with teargas and rubber bullets. At a news conference, Joe Prude says, "I placed a phone call for my brother to get help. Not for my brother to get lynched."

In the year after George Floyd's death, under pressure from the 3/20 Coalition, State College police names the three officers involved in the call leading to Osaze's death: Officer M. Jordan Pieniazek, Sgt. Christopher Hill and Lt. Keith Robb.

In the year after George Floyd's death, we add to the list more names of black Americans killed by police—so many names—such as: Jacob Blake in Kenosha, Wisconsin; Andrew Brown, Jr., in eastern North Carolina; thirteen-year-old Adam Toledo in Chicago; sixteen-year-old Ma'Khia Bryant in Columbus, Ohio.

While the trial of Minneapolis police officer Derek Chauvin is underway, on April 11, 2021, Daunte Wright is shot by police during a routine traffic stop in Brooklyn Center, just north of Minneapolis, a few miles from the courthouse where Chauvin is standing trial.

Police call the shooting "an accidental discharge."

The chief explains: "It is my belief that the officer had the intention to deploy their Taser but instead shot Mr. Wright with a single bullet."

Protest compounds protest until it becomes one big wail.

At the trial of Derek Chauvin in April, the first words the jury hears from the prosecutor are: "His name was George Perry Floyd, Jr."

I am driving home from work on April 20th when I hear the live coverage on the radio of the judge reading the jury's verdict, delivered less than eleven hours after the trial ended. I can hear papers rustling as the judge prepares to read from them, and the rustling in an otherwise silent courtroom ramps up my body's tension. My hands grip the wheel; tears are poised at the ledge of my eyes.

Slowly, one at a time, the judge reads each verdict:
Derek Chauvin is found guilty of second-degree murder;
Derek Chauvin is found guilty of third-degree murder;
Derek Chauvin is found guilty of second-degree manslaughter.

 Like many Americans listening, my body is holding and is ready to release the last few years leading up to that moment of conviction. I am holding the events of the previous month, when the 3/20 Coalition hosted Ten Days of Action, culminating in a daylong celebration of Osaze's life on 3/20, two years to the day that Officer M. Jordan Pieniazek shot and killed him.

That day, I go downtown for the celebration, and at a concert at the gates to the university, I sit on a curb, turn my face to the sun, and from behind my mask, I sing along to songs like "Waiting on the World to Change" and "A Change Is Gonna Come." Listening to Miss Melanie talk about our "beloved community" before she launches into song, I tap my feet and sing:

Justice for Osaze
We shall not be moved
Justice for Osaze
We shall not be moved
Just like a tree that's planted by the water
We shall not be moved.

■ ■ ■

Osaze was a religious man, churchgoing, and much more devout than I will ever be. I pray, but poorly, saying names and planting petitions as I go. The language in the readings for Pentecost in May 2020 were grim: God says "And I will show portents in the heaven above and signs on the earth below, blood, and fire, and smoky mist. The sun shall be turned to darkness and the moon to blood."

On Pentecost, I can see the divided red tongues of flame, hear the voices speaking in many languages, know how the holy spirit is supposed to break through the barrier of different tongues. In this moment, I can't worry about whether it's appropriate or appropriation for me to take African-American spirituals into my mouth. I send one up like a smoke signal into a sky already choking with smoke, a sky the purple of a bruise:

> When the clouds hang heavy and it looks like rain
> O Lord, how long?
> Well, the sun's drawing water from every vein
> O Lord, how long? ■

BLIND

Do you think it's strange
that I always dedicate
my poems to a blind man?
He lives in a cardboard castle
under the J railway.
When I hear
the high-pitched squeal
of train breaks,
I think of about his coat,
dusty and torn,
even when he's somewhere else,
like Wharf and Market Street,
begging for change. Scratch that.
He doesn't beg, he plays
his harmonica
for paying admirers, while
his eyes, no iris or
sclera, just brown clouds,
shift from side to side
like a metronome
measuring the song,
low and fragile,
that comes out of his instrument.

Does it seem strange to you
that, instead of turning my gaze inward,
I point it at the world,
changing people and objects
into things that I can praise?

Do you think it's strange,
blind man, that I talk about you
in the third person
as if you weren't here,
as if I were afraid
of opening my eyes, and seeing
who you really are?

JOSÉ ENRIQUE MEDINA

STRAWBERRY TIME

As the day turns toward fall
And the leaves of dogwood
Slowly redden, my mind leans
To the memory of wild berry,
Fragaria virginiana, tucked
Away as seeds after red was
Swallowed by the birds and
Scattered over waiting ground.
What is eaten in the present
Becomes fruit for the future,
As quantum time reminds
Us that all circles begin here
And now and what we do
Will ripple sweet or sour
And become the flower to feed
Or starve the coming generations.

CASSIE PREMO STEELE

WET JULY

The buzz of the leaves and the hum
of the air, summer where the seasons
slip past spring, slow in the heat and stop there
where locust shells cling to the trees
and the spilled chlorophyll quiver
cloudburst rattling the moringa.
No one knows you, how
the tongue clings to a mouth of cotton
when you try to breach an explanation.
No one knows you here, nor there
weather or tear, the cream soda
you sipped through sunburns
and secret lives bared between teeth
screeching tires of the trucks that spun
when daddies grew petulant
threw glass sacrifices
to the roads but you know
when the sky fades to the shade
of an infancy draped hydrangea
that the rain will drive the mimosas down
and the wrens will bathe and flick their wings
stop there, then fly away.

ELIZABETH ESTOCHEN

ROBERT GIPE

Robert Gipe is known in the region as a literary raconteur who manages to make readers and listeners laugh one minute and be moved the next with his witty, emotional, and propulsive writing and storytelling. His trilogy—*Trampoline* (2015), *Weedeater* (2018), and *Pop* (2021)—is a collection of connected novels that do much to expand notions of contemporary Appalachia and to always home in on the complexities of the lives of everyday people up against extraordinary circumstances.

Gipe grew up in Kingsport, Tennessee, but now lives in Harlan County. From 1997 to 2018, he directed the Southeast Kentucky Community and Technical College's Appalachian Program in Harlan, Kentucky. He is a producer of the *Higher Ground* community performance series, and has directed the Southeast Kentucky Revitalization Project. He coordinated the Mountain Mural Mega Fest, and is involved in a number of community-building and community-organizing efforts throughout the region. Novelist Silas House, who has known Gipe since he started writing, recently sat down with him to talk about his work, particularly his latest book, *Pop*, which was released in February by Ohio University Press.

■ ■ ■

SH: *Pop* is the final installment in your trilogy that began with *Trampoline* back in 2015. Tell us about the trilogy.

RG: The trilogy started with *Trampoline*. In that one the narrator is Dawn, who is telling a story about when she was fifteen and kind of got caught between an environmental activist grandmother and a mother who was dealing with substance abuse issues. Dawn was just trying to figure out how to grow, to find her own way. In the second book, *Weedeater*, she's older and her mother is having a harder time. That one is set in 2004. Here in Harlan, that felt like the roughest year in the opioid crisis to me. [*Weedeater*] is narrated by two people: Dawn and a local man who mows her aunt's yard. He's the weedeater of the title and he's in love with Dawn's aunt. This third book—the new one, *Pop*—is set in the run-up to the 2016 election. Dawn is telling a story about when she's

Robert Gipe

thirty-eight. She has a daughter, Nicolette, who's in high school, and they both narrate, and also Dawn's uncle, Hubert, who has been in all three books, narrates.

SH: So the trilogy covers a pretty wide canvas of years in the region.

RG: I've been alive fifty-seven years and I've been in Eastern Kentucky over thirty years, and the kind of Appalachian cultural movement that I arrived at when I came to Appalshop, and the Appalachian movement as it exists now, are different. When I first started teaching at the community college, every student I had would have some personal link to someone in their family or community to when coal mining started in Harlan County and that's no longer true. People can't look back to the beginning of that era. It feels in some ways that the culture is turning the page to a new generation, and *Pop* is an exploration of that—of the older generations and younger generations, with Dawn in the middle.

SH: You have these really vivid characters who have become beloved, vivid figures in Appalachian literature. How did you go about creating them?

RG: I was involved in theater in our community, a lot of oral history-based work. In 2003 we worked on a play [*Higher Ground*] that was a response to the opioid crisis, and in the course of my students interviewing others and my students talking to me, I heard a lot of young women's voices that were trying to process what was happening. I first went to [the Appalachian Writers Workshop at] Hindman in 2006 and I was in your class that year. The first fiction I wrote was my entry to Hindman, and *Trampoline* came out in 2015, so that was nine years in the making. In that time I had several younger students who worked in our office that were Dawns of a kind, so by the time the book came out she was based on so many different people that she really did become her own person.

SH: To me there's a Huck Finn quality to Dawn that makes her so memorable. All of your characters are. One thing that makes them memorable for me is the way you capture the dialect. It's a fine line to walk because if you don't do it just right it can come off like *Hee Haw*. So how do you strike that balance?

RG: I think it's because they're embedded in action. Something's happening to them or they're trying to get somewhere or they're trying to do something, so they're not thinking about how they're talking. They have too much going on in their lives, and they're in the community. I never thought of that before—but most of the situations in these books, they're among people that they're not self-conscious around. So it's that combination of knowing what they sound like, having a good strong idea of what words they do and don't use, plus being true to their emotions. It's the language we know and hear every day, so it's in service to what's going on in the book.

SH: One thing that makes your books unique is that they're illustrated, and you do those illustrations. They're not quite graphic novels, but they're also not just illustrations—the pictures are actual parts of the story and not meant to be looked at off-handedly. Can you talk about that process?

RG: I had just about given up around 2010 or 2011. I couldn't get the rules right, so I started making little zines, little sixteen-page chapters. I thought, *well, I'm going to just do it the way I want to*, and that's when the drawings came in. Then those chapters were serialized in the [online literary] magazine *Still: The Journal*. I was very interested in first-person narration and I loved the idea that the drawings could reinforce the fact that this was a person speaking to you. The drawings served as a kind of a middle place between the page and a film, where you're seeing someone talking. I love doing the drawings. That's a big part of my identity.

SH: I have some of those zines that I bought on that back table at the Hindman Settlement School. The illustrations also give the book a cinematic quality. I know that you're someone who loves cinema, so I wonder if you're the kind of writer who sees it all in your mind when you're writing.

RG: I definitely wanted it to be accessible to my community college students. I wanted a lot of—in *Trampoline* especially—car chases and a lot of mayhem that would make action sequences that would propel you. And I wanted to use the language of TV and movies, in terms of tropes and such. A teacher I spent the most time with, Darnell Arnoult—she always taught us to generate scenes. Scene after scene after scene, which is a pretty cinematic approach to writing.

SH: You tackle big issues in your books: environmental devastation, the fight for environmental justice, labor issues, drugs. Yet you don't allow the issues to overcome the human stories that are at the hearts of the books. How do you do that?

RG: When I set out on this, I had been around activism and I had found it very dramatic. It seemed to me that so many of the people who cause fiction to be in reader's hands—that whole conglomerate of people—that there was some idea among them that activism and the big issues aren't personal, and that ordinary people aren't involved in fighting for a more just world. But activism occurs in the context of a life—you still had to eat, put food on the table, go to family gatherings, and everything else. Really, when I thought I had a book was when our KFTC [Kentuckians For the Commonwealth, a statewide social justice organization] chapter was involved in protecting the water at the highest point [Black Mountain] in Kentucky. We met every week. That was an experience—and one that I and community members were in the middle of. Plus, Oxycontin hit.

The first lesson you get taught about plot is to create a good character; put them up in a tree they can't get out of, then set the tree on fire. So, the environmental crisis was the tree and the opioid crisis was the fire. I grew up in Kingsport, where there was a chemical company that made the chemical that went into the water in Charleston, West Virginia, that caused that crisis. In *Pop*, Dawn's husband, Willet—Nicollete's dad—was working for the company and delivering that chemical. When I was growing up my whole family worked for that chemical company. I've tried to do that in every book: have some kind of environmental crisis they're dealing with on top of everything else.

SH: You've done quite a bit of work in theater, especially community theater, which is such a specific and interesting concept. Tell us about *Higher Ground* and the way that has worked.

RG: It was born of the opioid crisis. Our first play was a collection of oral histories we collected and put together [in 2003], then we worked with professional theater artists to make an Oxycontin musical called *Higher Ground* in 2005.

I've kind of stepped back more into an advisory role and we've hired new folks to run it moving forward. Our latest one is called *Shift Change*. We worked with a director from the West End of Louisville [and] a choreographer from the Southside of Chicago. We had a Black Lives Matters demonstration in Harlan back in 2020, so we're unpacking that in the play, and connecting that to the erasure of one of our most vivid Black communities in Harlan County in the seventies. It also looked at Covid deniers and the political turmoil [of the past several years]. It was a lively play.

SH: What are the last couple of books you've read that you'd like to recommend?

RG: *Hillbilly Hustle* by Wes Browne. I was completely knocked out by *Every Bone a Prayer* by Ashley Blooms. I think it's great. Leah Hampton's *F*ckface*. I loved *The Secret Lives of Church Ladies* by Deesha Philyaw. I also love Kiese Laymon's *Heavy*, and a lot of his commentary in his essays is amazing. I've loved *An Indigenous Peoples' History of the United States* by Roxanne Dunbar-Ortiz. It's a history of the United States, but through indigenous eyes, looking east instead of looking west. Karen Salyer McElmurray's new book, *Wanting Radiance*, is great, and Charles Dodd White's new novel [*How Fire Runs*] about white supremacy is great. And *Even As We Breathe* by Annette Saunooke Clapsaddle—I'm a slow reader, but I read that book faster than any book I've read in a long time. ■

SECOND DATE

The table connected us, its flat plane
A continent of wood. You on one coast
I on the other, prairies of food between.
And I, reaching for the salt and pepper
Almost brushed the back of your hand
Which you drew back, not in dislike,
But perhaps sensing the lighting that might
Arc fingertip to finger if they touched.
I drank it all in, this indoor island,
Like the water I sipped nervously,
Wishing only that I had the courage
To simply reach out, discover your hand.
While above the continent, airy words
And smiles, the weather of our table-talk,
Rolled and mixed like summer breezes,
The scent of your breath a spice from the East.

ANDREW GUDGEL

IN THE SPRING WHEN MY BELOVED IS AWAY

> *yo / smell is*
> *always with me.*
> *—Sonia Sanchez*

On days I miss you,
I smell like a ginseng leaf

during the first rain after six
days of sun. And like ginseng,

I've hidden myself away
in this thin crease, high

on the mountain, but still
my missing you finds me

like a bear finds a bee-tree's
body and claws the comb's

belly like missing claws
mine. I pluck from beneath

blue cohosh a piece of the comb's
belly that the bear forgot,

and now I rush, like all bears
I've frightened from bee-trees,

down the mountain to wait
for your return.

NOAH DAVIS

THE HUSBAND TREE

DEVON CAPIZZI

M y daughter is working, early, in the yard. I hear her footsteps from my bedroom, my windows overlooking the teardrop of grass and the ring of hostas and ferns, the Japanese Maple on the very edge of my property. It's been this way all summer. She's left her job, moved home to be a gardener. My gardener. Soon, her shoveling will start and I will not be able to sleep again. The cleaving: it's too much, too rhythmic. *Thwack, thwack, thwack.* I get up.

Peering out the window, I can see only the back of her: a grey T-shirt sweated through already in the shape of a racer back sports bra, the chicken breast curve of her shoulder blades, the slightly tilted bend of her spine—she has always favored her right for some reason. The nape of her neck is shaved clean; her hair is short. Her legs, bent now as she kneels in fragrant mulch bedding, are muscled and tanned. She wears hiking boots every day. There is a baseball cap resting backwards on her head and I can just make out the knitted design of her old hockey team logo. Underneath: her loose curls—which she gets from me— and underneath those curls she is a mystery.

My daughter quit her job. A good job in the city that paid her well, awarded benefits. My husband and I never thought she'd have insurance past the age of twenty-six—she studied writing in college—and then a newspaper of all places gave her a salary, health insurance, paid vacation. All of that gone now with the simplest of explanations: *I just couldn't do it anymore.* She showed up two months ago with a duffle bag, a brown, open-faced box, her old Saab parked askew in my driveway. I didn't say a word, just opened up the door, let her in, and helped her unpack her things into the spare room.

In the yard, the grass is soft beneath my feet and sinks a little. July has gone muggy with humidity; I understand why she starts her work so early. I just don't understand the work itself. Years of writing late into the night, reading tirelessly through summer vacations, studying the classics, going to some small liberal college up north—my daughter wants to be a landscaper. I suppose there are worse things in the world than a lesbian landscaper.

"Morning," I call, as my daughter's shovel jabs the mulch. She leaves it there, the handle sticking up.

"Oh," she says, turning. "Hey."

Her work continues.

"What's it today? Morning glories? Geraniums? Little spruce trees?"

My daughter sighs and leaves her shovel in the ground again. "What do you want, Mom?"

"Nothing, nothing," I say, sounding light, I hope. "Just saying hello."

I stand behind her, admiring the Japanese Maple. Its bark is shiny in a way that makes me want to slide my fingertips all over it. Its branches are delicate; it is young, new, planted by my daughter just this summer. She says it won't get too much bigger. Still, it will give enough shade to the yard. I hear her grunt a little in the mulch bed; she works herself too hard.

"You need a drink or anything?"

"I'm fine," she says.

"I have iced tea in the fridge, unsweetened. And there's soda in the garage."

"I know," she says. "I'm fine, thanks."

Her arms keep working. She is making a neat row of identical divots, aesthetically pleasing.

"I can make some coffee," I say.

A forceful sigh, and she plants her shovel yet again in the mulch. "You want me to have a coffee with you?"

"Oh, no," I say. "I was just saying. I can brew a pot. If you'll have some, too."

The length of her forearm runs across her forehead, nudging her baseball cap so I can see the light red spots left by the adjustable clasp. She really shouldn't wear it like that.

"There's always the Keurig, too," I say. "If you don't want any, I'll just make a single in the Keurig. It's really no issue."

More digging. I notice now a small plastic skid of potted flowers sits beside her, just by her bended knee. Purple, gold, orange. They're beautiful. My daughter wipes her face again, this time with her shirt pulled up and over her face. She rests back on her legs, breathing deeply.

"No, no," she says. "I'll have a coffee."

■ ■ ■

In the kitchen, my daughter plates the meal with care. Two slices of golden brown toast with too much butter (the way I like it). A rugged terrain of scrambled eggs like a yellow mountain range. Two links of breakfast sausage—each. My daughter, so meticulous since birth. There is a smudge of dirt left on her cheek, her cheek pink from sun and work. I resist the urge to wipe it with a moist towel. In the cool of the central air, she wears an old hoodie from her high school field hockey team and there are holes in it. I have, too many times, offered to darn them. She has, each time, refused. Mothering, I have learned, is an exercise in restraint.

"Thank you for the breakfast," I say and smile at her. I try not to show just how pleased I am. "It's nice to have you home."

Her smile falters and wanes. "Well," she says. "It's not forever, but—it is nice. Thanks, Mom."

I smile, again. "What should we do?" I ask.

"We should eat," she says simply.

And so, we do. We eat together on the porch. The dog settles in between us on the floor, panting. The dog, a rescue chestnut hound, loves to be outside. His name— enigmatically—is Cartridge, as in ink. We call him Cart. My daughter loves him without borders. She pets his head, caressing his slim face.

"Are you a good boy?" she asks. "Are you a handsome pup?"

I pile eggs on toast and take a bite: buttery, silky, nourishing. I watch my daughter and the dog. She sneaks him bits of people food, I know. I know she does this, even though I tell her not to. I tell her: you will make him into a bad dog. But my daughter's love transcends—she will feed him bits of people food, she will pet his grumbling belly, she will kiss his velvet snout.

Privately, I want this kind of love from her. Her hands in my hair, her devotion. I want her to sneak me private things, small pieces of her meals. I want her to look at me and say, "Aren't you beautiful? Haven't you been good today? Aren't you a good little mother?" I want—I don't know what I want.

"Hey," she says.

I look up, startled. "Huh?"

The look on her face is one of pain, concern. It is alarming.

"What is it? What's wrong?" I ask.

I wipe my face with the napkin in my lap. I smile, shrug, as if to suggest the tears are not my own, that I did not play a part in making them.

"You're crying," she says, nodding in my direction, gesturing at me.

I brush a hand across my cheek and my fingers come away wet.

"Oh," I say. "Oh, how silly."

I wipe my face with the napkin in my lap. I smile, shrug, as if to suggest the tears are not my own, that I did not play a part in making them. Crazy, right? Where did these come from? I settle deeper in my wicker porch chair. Smile, always smile. There is a nice breeze now, though the air is getting hotter, heavy as a wetted blanket. I return to my plate. My daughter eats, slowly, in silence. At least, I think, she is feeding me, too.

■ ■ ■

At night, my daughter insists on sleeping in the upstairs guest room. She needs, she says, to be alone when she sleeps. I wonder at this—is it true? Is she hiding something? Is it me? In bed, I lay awake with Cart. He is thin and chilly in the cool, night air. I wrap my arms around him, but he does not feel satisfying. He is too thin, his ribs showing on the long, curved flat of his side. Still, I consider, in a way he is perfect—he's my dog.

Cart and I found each other in tragic circumstance. My husband had been dead two weeks (car accident, drunk driver). I was not sleeping well. I was eating nothing but peanut butter sandwiches to calm my stomach, not yet for hunger. One morning, the milk in our refrigerator had gone sour and clumped, so sludge-d and forgotten it brought fresh tears to my eyes. I am now a woman, I thought, who allows her milk to rot. I steeled myself. My daughter was not home with me. Alone, I got in the car. I drove.

On the way to the store I found an inlet for distraught vehicles and pulled over. I looked out. We lived and still live in a county so sparse and fielded it appears, at first glance, abandoned. Were it not for dots along the horizon—a far-off tractor tilling in the field, a silo filled with wheat, the single light gone on at dusk in a distant farmhouse—one might imagine this place a rolling expanse of emptiness.

I looked out the window and saw nothing but the cropped stalks of corn, their color waning from true green to an unattractive greyish brown. Slowly, my eyes dried. I felt the size and weight of myself at the sight of it all. These fields. Their width and breadth enveloped me; the color, washed of vibrancy, soothed my shaking hands; I became calm. In the distance, I saw a man and a dog trotting through the field. The man wore a rigidly brimmed straw hat, a solid purple button down, simple black pants—Amish. The dog, I could tell, was young. They were not working. They were out and enjoying each other's company. It was, the two of them, the only living thing that marked the land.

I did not buy milk but kept on driving. Cartridge was the only dog left at the animal shelter. He came home with a leash and a thin winter dog jacket. Love is so easy to give to something that will surely love you back. That first night we played fetch all through the house with a pair of my husband's old socks. I don't think he would have minded.

I wrap my arms tighter around Cart's body. He fidgets only once, then gives into my embrace. I picture my husband. Tall, rounded in the middle, like a baby whale made vertical, given legs to walk on. His hazel eyes and the soft red of his cheeks after a glass of wine with dinner. His hands large and decisive—tugging at my sleeve to get my attention, like a boy in the supermarket with his mother. His feet spread outward, flat and smooth—he had slipped so many times on our new hardwood floors. His shorts: cargo. His T-shirts: pocketed, Costco brand. His lips—they are my daughter's lips. I hug Cart tighter. He is asleep already. We are, I remind myself, two living things that mark this space. Together, in my king-sized marriage bed, we sleep.

■ ■ ■

It is not the shovel but the mower that wakes me in the morning. It is so early my head hurts, protesting consciousness. Cart is curled under the covers; he will not budge. Reluctantly, I swing my legs over the edge of the bed. I stretch, arms up over my head. I yawn, eyes watering, spit sprayed. My feet just graze the floor and it is cold. Outside, I can see the sky is candy blue and wisps of cloud drift in and out of view. The edges of neighbors' trees border my window. Leaning forward, I see her: my daughter, expertly operating the old hand mower she revived on her return.

I grumble down the stairs. I put the coffee on to brew. I check the dishwasher—I forgot to run it the night before. I purse my lips, roll my neck—remember to breathe. I breathe. I turn it on and go out on the porch where I can watch my daughter, her arms like chicken wings pushing the mower back and forth all through the yard. When she was little, my husband killed a cluster of baby rabbits this way. She had cried for weeks after. He had cried too, privately, only to me. He was soft, like a tender peach ripe for picking. But to our daughter, he showed only his solid, sturdy pit; he never wanted to bother her, to upset her with his sadness, his grief, his guilty feelings. And over time, I noticed she took to this, too, not allowing him to see her cry, only ever showing him a happy face, a playful nudge against his body. A couple of beers cracked open on the porch. Pistachios shelled for each other and popped, salty and dry into the mouth. They laughed a lot.

"Hey," I call out, waving my arm to get her attention. She is wearing his old ear muffs. "Hey!"

Her face flickers. She looks around, then sees me standing there. A single finger raised: hold on a second. I sit down on the porch steps and stretch my legs out so my feet rest in the freshly cut lawn. The sun feels good so early in the morning. I let it soak my skin. I close my eyes. I am almost asleep again by the time I hear the mower sputter to a stop. I open my eyes to see my daughter—sweaty arms bared by rolled-up T-shirt sleeves, the flush of her cheeks (so like his cheeks), the bouncing gait of her stride. She takes the ear muffs off and lets them hang from the back of her neck.

"What's up?" she asks.

"It's seven o'clock in the morning," I say. "Did you have to mow the lawn?"

"It needed it," is all she says, shrugging a little.

I look up at her. She doesn't quite meet my gaze. Two years on and there is still something dull in her expression. She is half dead or half stranger. She is not the lively self of yore—food fights in the kitchen baking Christmas cookies; heated arguments over the dinner table; the fire in her belly just after finishing a good book. *You have to read this; now, now, now.* She used to shove our hands full of battered paperbacks.

I slap my hands down on my legs and push myself up standing. "Okay," I say. "Sorry, okay. Do you want breakfast?"

She looks at me, but this time I deny all eye contact. "Sure," she says and drops her work gloves to the grass, wipes sweaty hands down the front of her shorts.

We go inside. I open up the fridge. I will make her breakfast today. My daughter will eat my food in my house. She will be the daughter. I will be the mother.

"What's the plan today?" I ask.

My daughter sits at the counter and swivels on a bar stool, still panting from the work and the heat. "Not much, actually," she says.

This is a turn. I extract the eggs from the fridge and start cracking them into a bowl. Usually, my daughter has a list a mile long of what she'll do, excuses, I'm sure, should I ask her to do something with me. We live again in the same house, but there is distance. It is very hard to lose a parent young in life. I read that sometimes, children will turn sour, subconsciously blame the living parent for being alive.

"What are you up to?" my daughter asks, sipping orange juice.

Where did she get orange juice?

"Oh, nothing," I say. "Just, hanging around. I'll walk the dog later if it isn't too hot on the paws."

My daughter chokes on her juice, then, cup removed from her mouth, I see she is actually laughing.

"What?" I ask, hesitant, unsure if I'm allowed to laugh, too.

"I don't know," she says, coughing, smiling. "'Hot on the paws.' Made me laugh."

"Well, I don't know why. The pavement can burn the shit out dogs. You have to be careful."

"I know," she says, smile waning. "It just sounded funny, okay?"

She has that look about her, the one resembling exhaustion—is she exhausted with me?

"It is kind of funny," I say, a sore attempt to save something happy between us.

We don't talk about my husband anymore. We don't talk about anything.

"I'm gonna go shower," she says. "I'll be down for breakfast, okay?"

She pecks me on the cheek, strides down the hallway; I hear her bounding up the stairs. And just like that she leaves me feeling like a failure, as if something I caught has been taken from me, as if an award has been stripped from my neck. Empty. I feel empty.

I whisk the eggs. They spit hot oil in the pan.

■ ■ ■

At the dog park, my daughter is chatting with the owner of a Boston Terrier, a man in his mid-thirties. I wonder if she is flirting. She wears loose-fitting cut-off canvas pants, hiking boots, the damn field hockey hoodie. On her head: the baseball cap. She looks like a lesbian. To me, she looks like herself, but when I push myself outside of motherhood, she looks so obviously like a lesbian it seems the look must be very carefully constructed and impossible to miss. It's a little embarrassing.

But the owner of the Boston Terrier—bearded, broad-shouldered, taller-than-her—seems so intrigued their interaction cannot possibly be platonic, can it? I keep an eye on them. Could she, after all these years, be interested in a man? And what would that mean for us? I correct myself—for me. What would I do with a straight daughter? A vision of manicures and pedicures, a wedding in a church, a house with a yard and hedges, grandchildren. Grandchildren that look like us, like me. I turn to my side out of habit, but there is no one there. I clear my throat. It feels like I've missed a step down the stairs.

And just like that, Cart is nipping at a German Shepherd; they don't know when to stop. I call my daughter over to help us tear the dogs apart. The owner of the Boston Terrier hovers close behind the mess, guarding his own dog and still feeling some need to engage with the situation. But my daughter doesn't hesitate. She struggles in between the dogs, stumbling as their bodies swirl around her legs, fingering Cart's collar. In the process of separation, her hand gets bit. Not badly, though there is blood. She tugs Cart roughly by his collar and clips him to his leash in one fluid motion. I am astounded by her, this master wrangler before me. I can never shake the feeling of my daughter as a child; she's still so young.

"Are you okay?" I ask.

She sucks fresh blood from the wound on her hand and I wince.

"It's fine," she says, tone sharp. "It's okay, but we should go." She turns from me to face the dog. "Come on, Carty," she says, patting his sun-warm ribcage. Her tone is soft with him.

I swallow hard and follow them.

In the car, I hesitate. I hold myself in. I am driving, steady and strong. I want to ask my daughter how she's feeling. I want to ask if she is okay, again. On her hand, the bite is turning black and blue. I want to ask so many things. There is a silent waterfall between us made of questions.

Do you need money? How long will you stay with me? Why did you leave that job? Why did you run from the city? Was it the girl? The one you were seeing with the nose ring? Did she break your heart? Is your heart still broken? Are you missing your father? How often do you think of him? And what do you feel when you think of him? And is it strange for you to be here with me, only me? As it is strange for me to be here with you, only you? And where do you keep your urn and do you ever hold it? And did you love him more than you love me?

I settle at a red light. My daughter sighs. Cart is stretched across the seat behind us. The air is so impossibly still. The radio is on and quietly humming something I don't know. My

I want to ask so many things. There is a silent waterfall between us made of questions.

daughter lifts her feet to rest on the dashboard, leaving marks there. I say nothing. The light turns green. I pull forward. I think sometimes his death has cheated me. The suddenness of it has made it nearly inconsolable, as if we may never recover. It is so drastic a change. I do, I admit, feel cheated. Not merely by the loss of it myself. I feel cheated, too, by the way it has changed my child, how the loss has taken her from me. How she no longer thinks of me the way she used to. How she no longer sees me. My daughter, she is here with me. But she is guarded now, and strange. I want to shake her. I want to tell her I am still here. I may not be the one she is looking for, but I am now the only one she has. I feel, far more intensely now, the way I felt when she spoke her first words: *Dada*, instead of *Mama*. My husband, I remember, had gloated.

"How's your hand?" I ask to break the silence.

"It's okay," she says.

"Liar."

She sighs. "It hurts."

"We should go—"

"I'm not going to a doctor."

My lips purse. Why are young people so averse to going to the doctor?

"Were you flirting with that man back there?" I ask, changing the subject.

"What," she says, half laughing.

"It just looked like you two might be getting along."

"I wasn't flirting," she says firmly.

"You were smiling a lot."

"We were getting along. We were talking about dogs."

"It looked like you were flirting."

My daughter adjusts herself in her seat. At first, I think she might crawl into the back to get away from me. She seems genuinely annoyed now. Why can't I ever let anything go?

"I don't mind that you were flirting, you know." I adjust my grip on the steering wheel and signal a left-hand turn. "It's okay with me, if you—you know, many people date both genders."

"Jesus Christ." My daughter wraps her hand in tissues from the center console. "I wasn't flirting with him. Full stop. Can we please stop talking about this?"

"Can I ask you a question?"

"You seem to be on a roll right now."

I eat the pain she causes me. "Well—how are you?"

"What?"

"I mean, really. How are you, really?"

The car is making a funny sound I have to call about. I will not bring it to the dealer this time. In my widowhood, I have learned the hard way. Too expensive. I turn again onto a road near home. We make it through a second light.

"Bad," my daughter says, simply. The word is easy, redeeming as an exhale.

At our road, it occurs to me that in the car we cannot escape each other, so I keep driving.

"I'm bad, too," I say.

"I know."

"You know?"

"Of course, I know," she says and still, I wonder how. My daughter settles deeper into the passenger seat, her feet propped up on the dash. She hugs her knees. "I worry about you."

I keep on driving.

I want to tell her she doesn't have to worry about me, but it feels like something too many people have said before. So much so that I end up saying nothing more at all. Instead, I keep on driving. Actions speak louder than words. Right now, I think, I am speaking with my actions: As long as I keep driving, that's how long I want to be close to you, trapped with you. We are in the fields again. The fields, they soothe. Perhaps, I think, this is the reason for all her gardening. All that dirt under her fingernails. It's like balm to a burn.

"Where are we going?" my daughter asks.

"I didn't know you worried about me," I say.

Her hand slides across the top spread of my back. A warm orange light spreads in through the windows, the sun a lowering blaze in the sky, the colors softer now like the smudges of an oil painting. My daughter's palm, calloused from her working in the yard, moves again across my back until it is no longer touching me. Her hands return to her lap and she is picking at the callouses now, and I want to tell her to stop that because it's really not good for the skin, to be picked at. At a fork in the road, I take the left-hand branch and the road carves a smooth slight curve through the sheep fields and we are in a one-lane covered bridge. It is dark inside the bridge, and you're supposed to make a wish in the very middle part of it.

My daughter says, "I worry all the time."

■ ■ ■

It's the middle of the night. I wake up and realize I still have hours of sleep ahead of me. And yet, I am awake. Cart is curled against my legs. He will not budge. I extend my arm to the still-made side of the bed and feel like a widow in a movie. I think: my person is gone.

Quietly, I make my way down the hallway to the guest room. The floorboards creak a little under foot, but I leave the lights off. If only, I think, to look at her. I'll be able to sleep again. At her bedroom door, I pause, lower the handle slowly, then push the door forward ever-so-slightly. It swings inward without complaint, no creaks, not a sound. It is a little frightening, actually, to know how easily and quietly someone could open this door. Would an intruder even wake us? I shiver. I enter the room on soft feet. If only to look at her.

But there is no one in the bed. I hear the shovel. *Thwack, thwack, thwack.*

■ ■ ■

"What the hell are you doing?"

My daughter is crouched, again in the bed of mulch that lines the edges of the yard. The yard, two months into her stay, is unrecognizable. Small flowers now line the curved edge of mulch. The green of the hostas and the ferns are black in the night, though some are illuminated by the moonlight, a glowing. The star-shaped leaves of the Japanese Maple cut dark shadows over the lawn. The grass is pristine, soft and buoyant. It is beautiful. In the middle of it all, my daughter crouches digging. She stops at my voice.

"Jesus fuck, you scared the hell out of me," she says.

"It's the middle of the night," I snap. "What is this?"

"I couldn't sleep," she says, as if sufficient.

I gape at her. "Warm milk. Honey and tea. Television. Heating pads. Those things help you sleep. This?" I almost shriek the word, gesturing wildly to the lawn that is no longer my dopey little lawn, the one that came with the suburban house. "This is insane."

"It helps me," she says.

"Helps you what? Forget about Dad? Work through your shit? Get over the career you threw away? This isn't you, Bug. This— this is insane. I can't do it anymore. I can't watch you do this."

My daughter takes a deep breath, releases it out so slowly. She gets up and turns from me, strides slowly into the dark.

"Where are you going?"

"Just a minute," she says.

I hear her crunch through sticks, dirt, gravel. She wraps around the house, disappearing for a moment. Then, suddenly, she re-emerges holding a small potted something. As she draws closer, I see it for what it is: a small tree in a small ceramic pot. She comes much closer to me than I expected her to; I nearly back away. She seems, in that moment, unrecognizable, as if I don't know her at all. And then, I look at her: her eyes are his eyes, her lips his lips. Her ears are entirely her own: big but soft, a little pointed. She makes that odd, half-smile expression of hers. She is my daughter again. She has a farmer's tan, I can see, just above her T-shirt sleeves. I shiver, thinking of the sun.

"It's—here," she says, handing me the pot and the small, particular tree.

The truth is that it is not quite a tree yet. It looks, to me, more like a single branch sprouted from the soil. Its trunk is curved like a snake and its leaves emerge in periodic clusters all along the irregular squiggle of "trunk." In its meandering, it is both long and relatively squat. The leaves catch my eye perhaps the most of anything, so dark in the night they must be vibrantly green. It is roughly the height of a stepping stool you might use in a kitchen to retrieve a bag of sugar from a higher shelf.

My daughter pulls at the back of her neck. Her eyes are fixed on the tree with such deep care it scares me. Has she really gone insane? I have allowed her to stay here, indulged

She comes much closer to me than I expected her to; I nearly back away. She seems, in that moment, unrecognizable, as if I don't know her at all.

her garden—have I enabled this insanity? Have I been missing the signs of breakdown?

"Explain," I say. "I don't get it."

"It's called a bio urn," she says, but her words are lost on me. "I took a small portion of the—remains," she says, uncertain of herself. Her words sound and feel labored, as if she does not quite know how to speak. Finally, she says, "I made you a tree."

We are quiet but for breathing.

"You made me a tree."

She nods. We look at each other, directly at each other. Together, we return our steady gaze the tree between us. I am holding a pot. Inside the pot there is soil and through the soil weave roots and from the roots this beautiful, delicate tree that holds small pieces of my husband's body. I think but do not say: it is a little bit like he's alive again. I am starting to understand. I am cool in my summer pajamas.

"I like working with my hands," she says, finally, breaking the silence. "It helps me. I miss him. I just couldn't sit at a desk anymore."

I think of sitting in my living room, the couch sagged on each end—mine and his. The empty place, the dent on his side of the armrest from where he pushed himself up each night for bed. It was too much, all that space. I got a dog to fill it in. My daughter built a garden.

My daughter clears her throat, sighs. "If you don't like it, I can't take it back."

Surprising myself, I laugh. I am in awe of her. Looking down, I see the ground is dug up in the middle of her garden.

"Is it ready?" I ask.

She wipes her face on the shoulder of her T-shirt. She is still looking at the tree. Then, she crouches to the hole, rounding it out one last time with her dirty hands. I see only the back of her. Her shoulders are wide and strong. Her curls are untamed and bounce with her movements. She is taller than me now, which is strange—when your children surpass you—but kneeling there in the garden, she still looks very small to me. There is a childlike wonder to her. There is energy in her body. She moves quickly and her movements are forceful. It strikes me that she looks a little angry. I understand this, too. Who knew anger could make something beautiful?

"Okay," she says, pushing herself up. "It's ready."

She takes the tree from me and I feel hollow in its absence, as if I might shatter at the slightest touch. And I watch as she carefully extracts it from its pot, placing it with the diligence of a new parent lowering a baby to a crib. When the tree is settled, she swaddles it in wet dirt and covers the patch with mulch. She stands and we admire her work.

"I kept it in my apartment," she says. "Two years."

I can't stop looking at the tree, this gift I am receiving. She, however, is letting it go.

"Was it always for me?" I ask.

She smiles. "I told you. I worry." She slaps her hand against her filthy shorts to get some of the dirt off. "Thought it might keep you company."

Reaching down, I touch the tree for the first time. It's a little rough. Carefully, I pluck a single leaf and hand it to my daughter. She takes it and places it in her pocket.

"You want some tea?" I ask.

My daughter laughs, rolls her eyes. "Okay," she says. "Okay."

■ ■ ■

Time, I learn, is endless. Time, I learn, is so close you cannot see it. And then, one day, something wrenches you backward. Everything unseen comes into focus. There it is, you think, this thing we call time. It is wide and flat and persistent as the fields. It is unmoving, and yet, still, it moves (tick, tick, tick). It is regular and strict, though it still manages to fluctuate (the darkness come at four p.m. all winter; the wash of sun at ten p.m. all summer). It is marked and felt differently depending on the person, and yet, we are all beholden to it.

I lie in my bed after the planting and my daughter—the smell of musty dirt and the sweetness of her sweat dried on her skin—sleeps next to me with Cart curled tightly by her feet. The sun is coming up outside my window, that pale orange light against the wall. Another day, another morning. I count my breaths, in and out, slow, unending. I fit my fingers in the notches of my ribs.

I have marked my time in varied units: how long has it been since we lost him? How long has my daughter chosen to been here with me, next to me, breathing slowly in and out? How many meals have I eaten alone in this house made strange in his absence? And how many sleeps with the dog in my bed?

I will mark my years with my husband tree. Every summer, I will measure him. I will count the curves in his trunk. I will survey each cluster of leafy greens, the waxy pads of green pinched lightly in between my fingers. And every week, I will prune his branches. I will give water to his soil. I will view him through the kitchen window, where, if I am so inclined, I might speak to him while I am doing the dishes. ■

ARGUS

On hot days I grow a little too complacent
being clever: like making love
and watching yourself making love
in your mind's dirty, happy eye
                    —that double exposure
when balance exceeds limits set
and you forget to stay inside yourself,
experience and meta-experience
not properly meshing   —do they ever?

These days, camera phones mean no
accidental double-exposure, no two-in-one
as spooled film nears its end but won't let go
of sprocket teeth, or thumb forgets to wind a knob
and separate moments join in time
ghosting together what never was:
            I'm thinking of the ancient 1940s
Argus 36 millimeter my father gave me
                    back before a boyhood trip.
            A black box as heavy as a brick
—never anything new in our flea market house—
            but oh,
                    what pictures that camera took!
A paperweight now, a roll of film
            still in it   —pictures of what
                    I could not tell you—
though each sharp snap of its single-reflex lens
made sure that boy knew this world depends
on light and dark working together.

                            KELLY McQUAIN

THE DEATH SPIRAL

In the
process of becoming
there is blood on the walls
a prophecy written in phoenix
blood spirits writhing inside
of one body, each begging
for bonding to the soul
that becomes you—
a faint ripple
of the Big
Bang.

ELIZABETH UPSHUR

PERSONA POEM OF THE SHAKESPEAREAN WITCHNURSE IN *A WINTER'S TALE*

I think but of Apollo, his sunned
visage bright as second winter stars to
gaze upon, methinks my queen was his true
equal a like as like to God enthrone-
ed. O even as the fair and gentle
Dian beside her too as sweet maiden
ness can boast was she, were she, will she be
if these lips, cold as frost did melt under
mine then, my own earnest embrace, lips to
lips, anon buried we her corpse all in
velvet thick as her beauteous rust mane
How like Persephone she lay as one dead, yet
hope I ere some livered strength such as men
may claim, is hers to the hilt and like a
falcon, held on Deaths dark gloved hand
she might rise to behold her castle keep.

ELIZABETH UPSHUR

PRACTICE, PRACTICE, PRACTICE

Sadness can be as easy-peasy
as walking past a glass display
of birthday cakes, as easy
as seeing two children made to
hold hands to cross a street,
as easy as watching your dog
lick a stranger. Sadness is easy
because it is the same thing
as happiness is unless you
take time each day to practice,
brush your teeth, smooth fear's lines,
smile ten times into the mirror.

JAMES RAMSEY

CHASING
THE TRAIN

RANDOLPH THOMAS

When the chimney cleaner arrives, Dad is scrounging in the drawer of a dresser, telling me he's sure he has a flashlight somewhere nearby. When I step to the door, the short boxy van is parked in the driveway. On the side of the van is printed *Chimneys cleaned, wood stoves installed.* The side door is open, and the chimney cleaner is already unloading his equipment, his long brushes wrapped in a tarp. He leans them against the van.

The chimney cleaner is tall and lanky, with a shock of thick reddish hair and a beard. When he comes in, he glances up at the high ceiling, the bare bulbs up there. He asks if there's more light, and I say that's all there is. The house was built in 1910, and my grandmother bought it in 1948. The electricity is original, the lights controlled by little round push-buttons on the walls. Someplace in all this mess are ornate glass covers for the light bulbs, if they are not broken.

The chimney cleaner nods. He's seen worse, I'm sure.

"Which one of you," he says out of politeness, because he knows. My dad opens his eyes wide, comically, and points a finger back at himself. The chimney cleaner is working for him. They shake hands and Dad introduces me. His son, the college professor, he says like there's a joke about it they've already shared.

We shake hands, and the chimney cleaner tells me his name, Roy. I try to read his face. I get the feeling he's trying to read mine too. He glances around again, at the moldy ceiling and the walls where torn wallpaper is hanging in dirty strips, and I see this as a good sign. I ask him if he's got enough room to spread out, and he says he thinks so. I've spent the last couple of hours clearing a path to the fireplace and an area for him to work, while my dad fumbled around, interrupted me, and insisted on looking at everything I touched like he was afraid I was going to throw something away. I've moved back the tables, unstacked boxes of books and magazines. The exposed floor, once lovely dark wood, is scuffed up and eaten away by termites. When I showed the damage to my dad, he said he hadn't known it was there. That's why he was looking for the flashlight, to get a better look at it.

Roy lays his brushes on the floor and unwraps them. He spreads out the tarp they're wrapped in to protect what's left of the floor, gets down on his hands and knees by the fireplace, and moves the filthy forgotten fireplace tools and the rack they sit in. He reaches in a bag and pulls out a surplus gas mask. I used to have one of those when I was a kid, that my dad bought me at the Army/Navy store. When he puts it on, I smell the old rubber and see through the dusty eye panes. The mask is tight on his face, the bands holding his hair to the back of his head. He looks like a giant insect with it on.

Roy uses one of his tools to jiggle the handle on the flue. When it opens, a billowing cloud of ash and what at first look like pine cones pour out. He sits back, raises an arm, and waves for us to get out, like we shouldn't be breathing this in, but we are both fascinated. The gray cloud rises all around us, filling the room to the dim ceiling, and I get a better look at what's poured out onto the spread, dozens of blackened, hardened carcasses of dead birds.

■ ■ ■

When I was little, the house belonged to my grandmother. She was a widow then, and I never knew my grandfather. When my parents and I drove into the city every other weekend, my mother and I stayed with her parents, in their house by the river, and my father stayed up here with his mother, to help her keep up the house, get to the doctor, or to do whatever else she needed, and I came over to visit and play during the day on Saturday. My other grandparents had lots of children and grandchildren, but my father's mother had only my father and me, and she indulged both of us, cooking for us, getting down on the floor to play with me.

But I never spent the night in her house, and even then, many parts of the house, especially the upstairs rooms, were shadowy and mysterious. Somewhere hidden in the upstairs rooms was a pair of spring shoes she'd bought for my birthday but was afraid to give me. Already, I'd hurt myself by falling from the magnolia tree in the back yard and landing on a root, and another time falling on a rock by the back fence. When that happened, she cried when she told my father and begged him not to tell my mother because she was afraid I wouldn't be allowed to come back.

Her house was neat then, with shelves in the living room filled with interesting books. She had a prism on the hearth, and in the afternoon we'd look for its rainbow to appear on the green walls like it had a mind and a schedule of its own. There were two glass-fronted cabinets in the dining room, one where she kept some of my father's toys, model ships he'd built in the 1930s, and another, a corner cabinet where I kept a few of my toys.

In the fifteen years since my father left my mother and moved in here, he's overrun the house with his hoarding, mostly books and magazines, rooms so full of them to the degree that the second floor sags, plus every piece of mail that's come to the house, along with various things he's bought at estate sales: a typesetting machine, a rock tumbler, a watch display rack he planned to arrange his gems and minerals on but never did. As my dad has gotten older, his hoarding and his poor decision making have gotten worse. After my grandmother's death, he inherited some money from her, and he spent a large portion of it building a huge garage on the back of the house. He can't drive anymore, but he keeps his car there. My wife believes he built it to facilitate his hoarding, and sure enough, within weeks he'd lined the walls with cardboard boxes.

I live a thousand miles away, and I visit him when I can. One day last fall, when we were talking on the phone, he complained about being cold. Why don't you turn on the heat? I asked, and he evaded the answer. Finally, he told me that the heat had been disconnected in the spring because he didn't want to pay his bills. I offered to pay all his bills for him online, but he didn't trust the system or me enough. He's always liked keeping his secrets and doing things his own way. It was a struggle to get his heat reconnected. I got the bills paid and called the energy company to send someone out to light the pilot, but the first few times he was gone when they got there.

Now he wants to install a wood stove, the kind that heated his home when he was a boy, in the living room. That's why he's cleaning the chimney, to run the pipe up there. I've told him it's a terrible idea, that the house, which is full of paper, will catch fire. He says he's sorry he told me about it, but I've come to town to be here when the chimney cleaner comes and try to talk my dad out of this idea.

■ ■ ■

The cloud of ashes drives us out the front door, which we prop open. The chilly air feels clean and fresh. I put on my jacket, and Dad always wears a heavy flannel shirt. While Roy works, we walk around the yard I used to mow when I was a kid using my grandmother's antique push-mower. Today the grass is brown and lifeless. The yard, except for my grandmother's cherry tree by the street, looks worn down and dying. The porch is lined with what's left of her boxwoods, thin sticks mostly. Some entire plants are missing. The house, white with green trim, is peeling and dirty. Dad keeps the windows shut in all weather, the shades pulled down or cardboard over them. He's taken out the porchlight by the door because he doesn't want people to see him coming and going at night. The neighborhood is quiet, safe, and comfortable, but he and my grandmother before him have never trusted the people who come and go from the long green apartment building across the street.

It seems like it's in our blood not to trust anyone, as my father doesn't completely trust me and I don't trust him. Our distrust has surely been exaggerated by his age and health, by the various distances between us, physical and otherwise, by this and other unhappy situations we've found ourselves in. It's strange standing on the front lawn with him while someone else is inside. Besides the rare repairman, I'm the only person allowed in the house. It's our cluttered palace of family secrets

Besides the rare repairman, I'm the only person allowed in the house. It's our cluttered palace of family secrets and ghosts.

and ghosts. Although I've been upstairs plenty of times over the years, the exact contents of the shadowy rooms up there are as much a mystery to me now as they were when I was a child.

While we wait, my father tells me a story in his long-winded, meandering way. During the Depression, when his family lived in a small town forty miles to the west, there was a train that crested the mountain, he says, carrying coal.

"I remember," I say, meaning the coal trains. I grew up only a few miles from the place he's talking about, thirty years later.

"You don't remember this," he says.

Boys in his town, he says, would chase after it. It slowed, he says, on the steep approach to the crest of the mountain. The fastest boy would grab hold of the train, climb on, out of breath, and throw coal down to the other boys. They'd run along beside the train and pick up the coal to take home to their families.

"Just imagine how dangerous it was," he says, "chasing the train in the dark, how brave these boys were." The boy on the train had to jump off before the train crested the mountain because afterwards it would start to pick up speed. If he missed his chance, he'd be in trouble, he'd be stuck on the speeding train, holding on as it barreled out of the mountains heading east.

He's told me this story so many times, like all the others. Why does he believe I have forgotten or that I haven't been listening? Maybe it's the onset of dementia, or maybe not; for a long time he's acted like he thinks my leaving Appalachia has eroded, or even erased, my identity.

■ ■ ■

Roy comes to the door and says he's finished. He's just cleaning up. He steps out on the porch and stretches his long arms, and we follow him back into the house. We leave the door open, and the room, kept closed tight and stuffy, is a strange mix of outside and inside. Where in this mess is my grandmother's prism, I suddenly wonder. Does it miss the wall it showed its magical spectrum on as much as I miss the magic? Dad and I stand in the cluttered living room and watch the chimney cleaner roll his brushes into the tarp. When he's finished, my dad shows him where he wants to put the stove, and describes—although they've already discussed it on the phone—how he wants to run the pipe up the chimney.

Roy nods and says it could be done, but he doesn't think it's a wise move, not in a house like this one. He taps his foot on the wood floor and says it's too dangerous. I must be panting with relief—I even put my hands together like a prayer. What he's doing is costing him money, sacrificing the sale and installation fee of a stove to do what's right.

I've written out a check from my father's checkbook and signed his name. I have it in my pocket as we walk outside to the van, Roy with his gear, and my father trailing along behind him. I take twenty dollars from my wallet and give Roy the check and a tip. My father starts talking suddenly about how, during the Depression, my great-uncle brought them leftover wood from a construction site to heat their house.

Roy listens, and I wonder what my father has said to him before, on the phone, and if he knew my father before that. My father says it's too expensive to heat houses these days.

"I heard that," Roy says.

I remind my father that he has heat in the house. I put my arm on my father's shoulder. I say, "You don't need to buy a wood stove, not in a house full of paper. It wouldn't hurt if we cleaned out some of that paper and moved stuff away from the heating units."

I'm hoping Roy will chime in. He nods and says, "Yep." I realize, too late, how professorial I must have sounded lecturing my father, and it makes me uncomfortable.

Roy shakes my father's hand, pats his shoulder. He shakes my hand and gets into the van. A moment later, he's backing it into the street.

We step up on the porch and survey the yard. My grandmother's cherry tree is holding winter tight in its unmoving branches, and the sky is bright in our eyes, enough to make an excuse for the squinting, distrustful looks. I'm sure my father sees this morning as a defeat, a disappointment, but he's not admitting it. He may or may not give up on this idea, the stove that can burn down the house and kill him, and I fear next time he will keep all his plans to himself, if he can remember to. I promise myself that I will listen carefully to what he's telling me, even if it's a story I've heard countless times before. I'll try to understand its true significance, to hear the intention behind the story, what he's not telling me.

He suggests we get some lunch, and I nod. He goes into the house to get his hat, and I follow him into the hazy living room where the colorless walls look like they've rarely been touched by light and the odor of ash still hangs in the air. The chimney cleaner has done his job, opened a door and closed it. Before leaving, he did us the service of sweeping up the dead birds, but he left the pockmarked floors streaked with ash. I go looking for a broom, but before I can find it, my dad has found his hat and is ready to go. He has the newspaper with him, the list of movie times, distraction enough to carry us away from our responsibilities here, and maybe that's for the best, for now. Some things here can't be fixed easily, and even some treasures may have to remain hidden, maybe for always. We leave the house the way it is, locked up, behind us, and head off down the sidewalk. ■

GARDEN HOE

It's not as sharp as it used to be. I hear
friends say the same of themselves, but I
believe that I've grown sharper through my years
of gardening, at least in ways that I
consider worthy. Now I notice where
my herb beds migrate to, and feed the dirt
accordingly. I've learned if nothing's there,
amend or move along. It never hurts
to sow for your own needs, plus more to share,
I've also learned. And how a drought can lend
you time to think and plan. How rain repairs
so quickly you forgive the wait. And when
to be as blunt as my old chopping hoe,
or when to plow loss under, let it go.

DANA WILDSMITH

OXYCODONE

Johnny sure would love to get
the hell out of here, but where
on Earth could he go? Here being
pain in the legs and hips
from the wreck. Here being surgery
bills that don't square with bank
accounts. Here is knowing the drunk
walked away unscathed. Here is
the torpor of this trailer behind

daddy's place. What separated me
from Christ's love, he says? Trouble
or hardship or persecution
or, or, or...
                          I am the voice
of one crying out in the wilderness
and only one power has released me
from this agony. Look at the trees,

he says. Look at the grasses, the river,
the whitetail. See how alive, how high,
how abundant.
                          If you fall asleep
it'll grow right over your head. Tell me
how ruin and want endure in a place
capable of this much green?

JOHN MARK BALLENGER

BOOK REVIEWS

Elizabeth Chiles Shelburne. *Holding On To Nothing.*
Durham, N.C.: Blair, 2019. 272 pages. Hardcover. $25.95.

Reviewed by Karen Salyer McElmurray

Years back, I heard a lecture by novelist Charles Baxter called "Making the Ordinary Extraordinary and the Extraordinary Ordinary in Fiction." *Holding On To Nothing*'s ordinary world is a small east Tennessee town. I've been gone for too many years from my own small hometown in eastern Kentucky, and the pages of Elizabeth Chiles Shelburne's debut novel take me back there with an ache I recognize. I know the world this book summons inside and out. Its sound of cicadas, "their steady, pulsating drone, punctuated by the maraca shakes of katydids." Its people, the church ladies with their casserole dishes. The town has its Walmart and an ammunition plant for jobs. There's also whiskey at Judy's Bar on a Saturday night, a place where music drifts out into the packed parking lot and loving makes the world fine, but just for a spell.

In the background of this ordinary world, one senses strictures about how life ought to be. There's the ought-to for women, for families, for living right. Gossip dies hard about hard-living families, and young women who make the wrong choices end up the subject of speculation, not to mention the consequences of their actions. It's that kind of ordinariness which at one point in my life sent me on as many highways out as I could find. I wanted more, be it via places or people or ways of seeing and believing that home wouldn't allow me. Wanting out—or not wanting out—is at the heart of *Holding On To Nothing*.

The central characters in Shelburne's page-turner are a product of such complex wishing. Lucy Kilgore tries "to live that dream" of heading to the city, to go to college, but also to find a happy ending. She keeps herself "moving forward, working hard, and caring about something" so she won't end up with nothing better than what she has. Lucy finds herself pregnant after one night when "whisky obliterated every objection she ordinarily would have had" and she ends up in the back seat of a Camaro with Jeptha Taylor, a talented mandolin player who "spends his days drunk and wild." Lucy clearly sees that "the wild joy of the moment [has] evaporated as quickly as rain off the summer sidewalk." Jeptha, who has loved Lucy since he was sixteen, knows well enough how lives can end up. His mother's dream was to "make the future something other than an unedited rewrite of the past." And there they are, their dreams playing out like a bad hand, bound to the ordinary worlds they have always known.

Back in my own eastern Kentucky days, I drank my share of bootleg whiskey and railed against the world that made me, but I also remember moments of such precarious beauty.

Rose-colored dresses at the thrift store for a quilt I made. The walls of a house I saw painted with scenes from the Book of Revelations. Sketching by a creek with a water-color artist I loved but couldn't have. Moments of beauty, tenderness even. I wanted more of those moments in *Holding On To Nothing*, be they in glimpses of the land or in snatches of conversation with elders. Sometimes the ordinary, the just-might but not quite in this novel makes me feel like I can't breathe. Jeptha just might be able to take on the terrifying responsibility of being a better man than the men he grew up with. That just might is a low-down country song on a humid summer night, the sound of those cicadas whirring from the trees through a rolled down car window. And that may be the point at the heart of this ordinary world.

In the end, though, songs are the thing that lift *Holding On To Nothing* up and make it extraordinary. When he's a boy, Jeptha hears a mandolin and the song "Shady Grove." He recognized "something magical in the high, forsaken sounds...fingers made against the pear-shaped instrument's double strings." That mandolin becomes his own, and it is when he plays it and sings his songs that he transcends his own self. Music sets him on fire like no other thing in his life ever has. Playing "one of those old songs," Jeptha feels power, sorrow, something truer than true, and Lucy sees that power in him as he plays. When Jeptha plays, he becomes another man, and the novel becomes a song—one about what family means and can't mean, what forgiveness is and wants so very badly to be. We need those transcendent notes in this novel of desire and sorrow and holding on. I, for one, am still hearing that music and knowing that where I come from is in my blood for good. ∎

Jesse Graves. *Merciful Days*. Macon, Ga.: Mercer University Press, 2020. 60 pages. Softcover. $16.00

Reviewed by Melissa Helton

Jesse Graves's fourth collection, *Merciful Days*, takes us to the poet's childhood, the landscape of east Tennessee, and the lives of his ancestors, both roving and rooted. This is familiar territory for Graves, but readers of his previous work need not worry about the repetition of prior collections. Like Monet creating many singular moments with those same waterlilies, Graves's returning to his family history and landscape  illustrates that writers can use the materials of their own lives to lift readers into discussions of belonging, loss, and the broader awareness of our transient part in humanity's story. These poems show that when we come back and meditate on those familiar images, we learn something more, because each time we come back, we are a little different. Indeed, the first line in "History" reminds us, "Every hour changes something forever."

Those new to Graves's work will immediately recognize his poems as accessible—in the best senses of the word. It's possible for the language to be simple because the images and poetic movements do the heavy lifting. Purposely obscure writing might make a clever puzzle, but that locks many readers out from deep interaction, and hyper-analyzing every piece's intent and meaning is perhaps why so many students dislike poetry after schooling. Dissection doesn't often encourage life.

As we gather the images in this collection, we hold mother's gingham dress, road-killed deer, the Challenger explosion, the North Star, a blue tractor. We walk slowly with the poet, ushered without need for dictionary or footnote. These poems are like putting tired feet in the creek, not like being handed a calculus exam.

Another of Graves's strengths is to fully characterize a person or a landscape with a small brush, such as in "Old Man Wandering the Roads" as the speaker describes a grandfather:

> *He left a trail of growing things wherever he went,*
> *and carried a little change in his pockets*
> *to prove he had done his day of work,*
> *maybe not a lot of it, but enough to get around,*

We see this in "Raft" with the succinct recollection, "And then I was different, sitting alone / on the raft of being twelve years old." Or in "Rocks," when the speaker and mother plant the garden while the father is out on the road:

> *We dug rocks with a hoe and a rake,*
> *scooped mounds of soil for bean-hills*
> *only to find more rocks underneath.*

These poems ground us in a specific time, with an object or a gone person, and then zoom us back to before time itself, or forward, past even the end of the poet's life when he becomes a gone person himself. Graves holds us in the verb of the present, but always with that wider context, as in "Mossy Spring" where the speaker drinks, calling forth the first peoples who drank here, then the trackers and farmers:

and now you, looking for the lost
kingdom of your ancestors, dousing
their eternal thirst to be found.

In the end, as folks with corporeal limitations, we experience reality one now at a time, with the past and future colliding around and in us. The poems in *Merciful Days* dance in that overlap between times, that awareness that this now is as temporary as all those past and yet to come. The ending of "Hawks," where the birds hover over a ridgeline "watching me, keeping cold eyes / fixed on all I thought was mine," finally brought to mind the feeling that had trailed me through the collection, the acknowledgement in "Zazen on Ching-t'ing Mountain" by Li Po (701-762 CE):

The birds have vanished down the sky.
Now the last cloud drains away.

We sit together, the mountain and me,
until only the mountain remains.

And if we step back and widen the frame even further than Li Po did, we have to admit even those mountains won't remain. In childhood, things can seem so eternal, so solid. As we age, we learn their impermanence, and our own. Some deal with that through existential dread and a mid-life crisis. Some deal by obsessing over a legacy. Some let go and float. Some drink a lot. Some write poems.

The specificity of these poems, how they bridge a simple hay bale to the wider realities of human time, is a good meditation for us all—and especially to writers who feel they don't have anything to write about. This book shows us that if we have lived a day of life, we have a poem to write.

The poems in *Merciful Days* seem well-digested and polished to the point there feels an insular space between the poet and the readers. Admittedly, I am a greedy, curious reader. I can't help but want to sit with the poet, neck-deep in the messier, less-processed parts of these experiences, not just the calm recollections of them afterwards. I can't help, after viewing the poet's summonings of the world around him, to want a few more vulnerable self-portraits.

After wandering through a field with Graves, listening to his stories about barn swallows, cows, and dead family members, we will feel more connected to each other and to our own lives. Indeed, every time we wander through a field with Graves, we will carry away something worthwhile. ∎

Charles Dodd White. *How Fire Runs.* Athens, Oh.: Swallow Press, 2020. 272 pages. Softcover. $22.95.

Reviewed by Randi Adams

By opening his latest novel with a swastika flag being hoisted into the air and a Nazi salute, "Seig Heil," proclaiming victory, Charles Dodd White warns us the stakes are high in the story to come—and he doesn't disappoint. *How Fire Runs* is White's fourth novel, and in it he expertly intersects race, social justice, small town politics, community, and environmental destruction.

A resident of Knoxville, White utilizes his understanding of east Tennessee to portray a contemporary fictionalized Elizabethton, a town tucked into the bounds of the tri-cities of Johnson City, Kingsport, and Bristol.

The first parts of the novel prepare the reader for a confrontation between Democrats Kyle Pettus, Gerald Pickens, Frank Farmer, and their allies, with Gavin Noon and his neo-Nazi followers. While they eventually clash ideologically in the debate between Farmer and Noon in the lead-up to the election for a seat on the county commission, this is not the climax of the story. This expert maneuver on White's part—one that left me wondering, *Well, what now?*—creates necessary chaos and builds a palpable sense of anxiety and suspense that drives the story through destruction and to its resolution. Though literary fiction tends to prefer characterization over plot, sometimes dragging the story along, White shines in his ability to maintain the story's momentum while developing the characters to their full portraiture.

The characters populating *How Fire Runs* represent a wide range of morality and ideology. Noon, leader of the "Little Europe" neo-Nazi compound, is irredeemably reprehensible. His physicality and sense of style, often involving suits and fedoras, make him a caricature of a villain, almost laughably so—except men like him do exist in the world, and the ideology they espouse is even more dangerous. Pettus is the obvious protagonist of the novel, but he is not Noon's antithesis. Farmer, one of few Black members of the community, is the closest this novel gets to a moral good. While he is dragged begrudgingly into the political arena by Pettus, Pickens, and other Carter County politicians who want to keep Noon out of power, Farmer ultimately decides to run against Noon out of a sense of responsibility and protection for his community, despite the fear of retribution from the white supremacists in the county, especially Noon's neo-Nazis. The diverse beliefs espoused by the characters, as well as the actions they take in lieu of these views, cultivate the true-to-life quality of the novel.

While White does not allow Noon a chance for redemption, Jay Harrison, one of Noon's initial followers, is ultimately redeemed. Throughout the novel, the reader is given a glimpse into Harrison's past and how he gets caught up in white supremacy through the need to survive his prison sentence. In a subtle way through Harrison's backstory, White critiques the way in which the prison system's cruelty strips people of their identities, sometimes contributing to the spread and exacerbation of violent, organized white supremacy. As Harrison's relationship with former love interest Emmanuel, a Black artist and marijuana dealer, grows, he begins to find the sense of self that prison stripped from him. It is this internalization that pushes him to leave Little Europe, resurrecting "Jay" and rejecting who he was as "Harrison."

White's storytelling blends evocative imagery and language with pithy directness and honesty. This balance contributes to his ability to present contemporary Appalachia with clear reverence without ignoring or excusing the problematic parts of the region's culture that would allow groups like Little Europe to take root and thrive. The only time I found myself questioning the novel's plot was when the conservatives on the county commission band with Pettus and Pickens to stop Noon ascending to power. Certainly, there are conservatives who would act likewise, but given the increasing tribalism of two-party politics, it took more effort to believe.

As is often true of Appalachian literature, even when a story isn't about the environment, it always slips into the forefront. Both Pettus and Farmer work closely with plants for a living, the former as a nursery owner and the latter as owner of an arbor business. Farmer's surname is certainly not coincidental. In the aftermath of the novel's climax—a tragic wildfire that destroys massive tracts of forest land, plant matter, and robs many of life—it seems White uses these associations with nature to portray Pettus and Farmer as new growth, the town's hope for a better future.

After the fire and defeat of Little Europe, Farmer points out that the same problems that allowed the community's acceptance of Noon still exist when Pettus tells him that people are calling him a hero. Farmer responds, "I think heroes are supposed to be loved…This place doesn't love me. Doesn't love me or my wife and girls…I'm convenient for this place, but being convenient means you're just a thing." Through Farmer, White confronts even the most well-intentioned white readers with some hard but necessary truths.

How Fire Runs faces down one of the most worrisome contemporary social developments, a phenomenon that, after the Charlottesville Unite the Right rally, is demonstrably problematic in Appalachia: the resurgence, expansion, and organization of white supremacist and fascist groups. In perhaps one of the most poignant lines of the novel, Jay finally rejects his ideology, telling Noon, "We all just want to find a way to ease the everyday hurt." The novel warns that it is through the transformation of fear and suffering into hate for the perceived other that kindles flames and allows fires to run. ■

SLIVER

Sledgehammered
   eighteen inches through hemlock roots—
surveyor's men sink rebar flush with the ground—
   a legal stake hostaging the boundaries of my life—

All triangulation
   and number, GPS assisted, true as an atomic clock—
with scientific jargon inked
   in equations and proven formulas. I do not doubt

the accuracy of the surveyor's angle, letters of the law. As an agent
of the state, he declares there can be no common ground—

   He knows the discrepancy, my thirty-five years'
residence in the county deed book— he bullies with his perfection—
   It is but a sliver—a long acute angle—and of a few marginal feet—
yet an insult
      a break-in—   a trespass—

a bludgeoning by an arrogant man—
I request that the iron be removed —he doubts it will go anywhere—

After many messy months, I have paid again for what I own—
I pry and yank out that rapier—
hoping the land heals as best as it can,

without a scar.

FREDERICK WILBUR

CONTRIBUTORS

Randi Adams received her Master of Arts in English from Western Carolina University in 2019. She has presented at the American Literature Association and Appalachian Studies conferences, among others, and is published in a forthcoming edition of the *Journal of the Short Story in English*. She is most interested in Southern and Appalachian literature and cultural history, especially in relation to economic class and the environment.

John Mark Ballenger lives with his wife and two children in Mount Vernon, Ohio. He grew up in rural southeastern Ohio, the northern edge of Appalachia. That landscape and people influence much of his writing and interests and imagination. John earned his MFA in poetry from Ashland University.

Devon Capizzi is a writer based in Brighton, Massachusetts. Their work has been supported by the Tin House Workshop, the Bread Loaf Writers' Conference, and a fellowship from Emerson College. Their writing has appeared or will appear in *Pigeon Pages, Ninth Letter, Foglifter Journal, Passengers Journal,* and elsewhere. When they're not writing, they're probably cooking.

Andrew K. Clark is a writer whose work has appeared recently in *Out of Anonymity: The UCLA Writing Project, Good Juju,* and *NO:1* journals. Main Street Rag Press published *Jesus in the Trailer,* his full-length book of poetry, in 2019. He is the recipient of the Georgia Southern University Roy F. Powell Creative Writing Award and is an MFA candidate at Converse College.

Noah Davis grew up in Tipton, Pennsylvania, and writes about the Allegheny Front. Davis's manuscript *Of This River* was selected by George Ella Lyon for the 2019 Wheelbarrow Emerging Poet Book Prize from Michigan State University's Center for Poetry, and his poems and prose have appeared in *The Sun, Southern Humanities Review, Best New Poets, Orion, North American Review,* and *River Teeth,* among others. Davis earned an MFA from Indiana University and lives with his wife, Nikea, in Missoula, Montana.

Elizabeth Estochen is a queer/non-binary writer and editor based in Charleston, South Carolina. Their work has appeared in *Emerge Literary Journal, Barren Magazine, Versification Zine,* and *Dirt Media,* and they are a first reader for *Ploughshares.* Their debut chapbook, *For Love, and for Cruelty,* was published in January 2020 by WordTech Editions.

Andrew Gudgel is a writer, translator and poet who lives in Maryland. His essays, poetry and translations of Classical Chinese poetry have appeared in *Lily Poetry Review, Speckled Trout Review,* Western Michigan University's journal *Transference, Brevity* magazine's blog, *Under the Sun,* and other publications. He is a graduate of Johns Hopkins University's Science Writing program and the Kenyon Review Writers Workshop.

Reshmi Hebbar is a writer and professor of multicultural literature at Oglethorpe University in Atlanta. Her nonfiction has been published at *Slate,* and her fiction has been published at *Funicular Magazine, The Account, Parhelion, West Trade Review,* and is forthcoming at *The Santa Fe Literary Review* and *The Chaffin Journal.* In 2020, one of her stories was nominated for a Pushcart Prize.

Melissa Helton is Associate Professor of English at Southeast Kentucky Community and Technical College. Originally from the Great Lakes region, she has called southeast Kentucky home since 2010. Her poetry, nonfiction, and photography has appeared in *Anthology of Appalachian Writers, Still: The Journal, Pine Mountain Sand and Gravel,* and more. Her chapbook *Inertia: A Study* was published in 2016. She has publications forthcoming in *Shenandoah* and her chapbook *Through the Interval* is forthcoming from Workhorse Press in December 2021.

Silas House is the nationally bestselling author of six novels, most recently *Southernmost,* as well as three plays and one book of creative nonfiction. He is a frequent contributor to the *New York Times* and *The Atlantic,* and his writing has appeared in *Time, Oxford American, Narrative, Ecotone,* and many other publications. House serves as the NEH Chair of Appalachian Studies at Berea College and on the fiction faculty at Spalding University's MFA in creative writing program.

Alison Condie Jaenicke teaches writing at Penn State University, where she also serves as Assistant Director of Creative Writing. Her work has appeared in or is forthcoming from such places as *Pleiades Magazine, Hippocampus, Superstition Review, Gargoyle Magazine, Storyscape Journal, Brain, Child,* and *Northern Appalachia Review.* Her essay "I Slept Well If You Slept Well," published in *Isthmus* Issue Number 4, was recognized as Notable in the *Best American Essays 2016.* Find her online here: https://alisoncjaenicke.weebly.com/

Karen Salyer McElmurray earned an MFA from the University of Virginia, an MA in Creative Writing from Hollins University, and a PhD from the University of Georgia. Her work has received numerous awards, including grants from the National Endowment for the Arts. She has published multiple fiction and creative nonfiction books including *Surrendered Child* and *Motel of the Stars.* An essay collection, *Voice Lessons,* was released by Iris Press in June 2021.

Kelly McQuain is an artist and writer whose prose and poetry have appeared in *The Grand Journal, American Poetry Review, Best New Poets, The Pinch, Kestrel, Spunk, Knockout, Painted Bride Quarterly, The Philadelphia Inquirer, Kin, MEAD, Assaracus,* and *The Harrington Gay Men's Fiction Quarterly,* as well as in numerous anthologies. His prizes include winning the *Bloom* chapbook contest for his chapbook, *Velvet Rodeo,* as well as fellowships from the Sewanee Writers' Workshop and Lambda Literary.

José Enrique Medina earned his BA in English from Cornell University. He writes poems, short stories, and novels. His work has appeared in *Best Microfiction 2019 Anthology, Tahoma Literary Review, The Burnside Review,* and other publications. He is a VONA (Voices of Our Nation) POC fellow.

Jeremy Paden was raised in Nicaragua, Costa Rica, and the Dominican Republic. He is a poet, translator, and professor of Latin American literature at Transylvania University in Lexington, Kentucky. He is the author of four collections of poems. Among these, *ruina montium,* about the 2010 Chilean mine collapse, has been published in both English (Broadstone Books, 2016) and Spanish (Valparaíso, 2018). He is also the translator for various poets from Argentina, Chile, Colombia, and Spain.

James Ramsey worked a variety of jobs including construction worker, librarian, mail carrier, disability evaluator, auditor, and fraud investigator before turning to his life's unfulfilled goal of writing creatively. In 2020, he was invited by *Arc Poetry Magazine of Canada* to participate in online mentoring in its Poet in Residency program. Also that year, his first published poem appeared in *Broad River Review,* where in 2019 he was a finalist for the Rash Poetry Award.

Cassie Premo Steele, Ph.D., is an award-winning poet and the author of sixteen books, including six books of poetry. Her work has appeared recently or is forthcoming in *Open Minds Quarterly, Sinister Wisdom, Oxford Magazine, Windmill, Lavender Review*, and *Cutthroat Magazine.* She lives in South Carolina with her wife, dog and three chickens. Her website is www.cassiepremosteele.com.

Randolph Thomas's short story collection *Dispensations* won the Many Voices Prize from New Rivers Press in 2014, and his poetry collection *The Deepest Rooms* won the George Cable Award for Poetry from Silverfish Review Press in 2015. His work has appeared in *Glimmer Train Stories, The Hudson Review, The Florida Review, The Common, New Letters, Pleiades, Poetry Daily, Verse Daily*, and many other journals. He teaches at Louisiana State University in Baton Rouge.

Elizabeth Upshur is a Black Southern storyteller, the Associate Poetry Editor for *Okay Donkey Mag*, and a Fulbright alumna. Her work can be found in *Augur, Pretty Owl Poetry,* and *Red Mud Review.* She is the inaugural winner of the *Brown Sugar Lit Mag* prize and recent *Gigantic Sequins* flash fiction winner. She tweets @Lizzy5by5.

Frederick Wilbur has authored three books on architectural and decorative woodcarving, and two poetry collections, *As Pus Floats the Splinter Out* and *Conjugation of Perhaps,* (forthcoming from Main Street Rag Publishing). His work has appeared in many print and online reviews. He is poetry editor for *Streetlight Magazine.*

Dana Wildsmith is the author of a novel, *Jumping,* and an environmental memoir, *Back to Abnormal: Surviving With An Old Farm in the New South*, which was Finalist for Georgia Author of the Year. She is also the author of five collections of poetry. Wildsmith has served as Artist-in-Residence for Grand Canyon National Park and will serve as Artist-in-Residence for Everglades National Park. She lives with her family on an old farm in north Georgia, and works as an English Literacy Instructor at Lanier Technical College. Her widely followed blog, http://www.danawildsmith.com/blog, focuses on the life of a working writer.

A Kentuckiana native, **Katelyn Joy Wilkinson** holds an MFA in Poetry from the University of North Carolina at Greensboro and currently lives in Las Vegas, Nevada. She teaches creative writing at the College of Southern Nevada. Her work is published or forthcoming in *Reed Magazine, 45th Parallel, 580 Split*, and *Passages North*, among others.

www.ingramcontent.com/pod-product-compliance
Lightning Source LLC
Chambersburg PA
CBHW070605180626
46817CB00005B/2001